SOMETHING TO SAY
TO THE CHILDREN

SOMETHING TO SAY TO THE CHILDREN

———————— · ————————

John R Gray

Edited by Sheila Gray

———————— · ————————

T & T CLARK
EDINBURGH

Copyright © T & T Clark Ltd, 1988

Typeset by Bookworm Typesetting Ltd, Edinburgh
printed and bound by Billing & Sons, Worcester

for

T & T CLARK LTD
59 George Street, Edinburgh EH2 2LQ

First printed 1988

British Cataloguing in Publication Data
Gray, John R. (John Rodgers), *1913-1984*
Something to say to the children.
1. Christian church. Children's sermons –
Texts
I. Title II. Gray, Sheila
252'.53

ISBN 0 567 29151 0

FOREWORD

This is not a book of talks for children ready for immediate reproduction from the pulpit. It is meant as a book of *ideas* for busy ministers.

I once asked a friend who was studying divinity how he was enjoying his course. He replied immediately, "I don't mind preparing the sermons, but oh, the children's talks! It's so difficult to think up ideas." My mind immediately went to the hundreds of children's addresses which my husband had produced during his forty-five years in the ministry. It seemed such a waste to leave them lying in a cupboard when they might be giving help to some harassed minister on a Saturday night. I have a mental picture of John, after a hectic week, sitting with a look of determined despair on his face, saying, "I'm not going to move from this chair until I've thought of something to say to the children tomorrow." The "something" – an idea – usually came. Sometimes he felt that he had not worked out the idea as well as he might have done (Sunday lunchtime is an hour of regretful afterthoughts in most manses!). But the idea was usually good.

I have made occasional alterations where very local references or phrases now out of date were used, but on the whole the talks are exactly as *spoken* to the children, hence the colloquial English and occasional verbless sentence, not something John approved of generally when writing. I hope he will forgive me! They do help to convey to the reader something of the laughter and love of children which shone through his talks from the pulpit.

I have tried to check for any errors. Another favourite pastime for the Manse Sunday lunch was 'Find the deliberate (or not so deliberate) mistake.' Where a text is quoted, the source is usually the Authorized Version or the Good News Bible, but occasionally another translation is used if the words are particularly apt.

John had profound respect and great affection for his fellow ministers. I would like to think that, although his voice is not now here to support them in life, he may yet speak to them through this little book.

Sheila Gray

CONTENTS

Foreword   v

THE CHURCH'S YEAR

CHRISTMAS
Jesus' birth certificate   3
Will Jesus be here?   3
The first chapter   4
Bicycle or tricycle?   5
The most important Christmas card   6
Christmas post   7
Find the baby   8
The first Christmas present   8
Chocolates   9

NEW YEAR
Just one more present   11
The diary   11
Visitors   12
The good companion   13
The new calendar   13

EPIPHANY
The Wise Men   15
Gold, frankincense and myrrh   16

THE FLIGHT INTO EGYPT
The spider   17

PALM SUNDAY
Palms   18
By appointment   19

EASTER
The cross which endures 20
To be continued 21
The end 22
Nobody Knows What 22
The Ascension 23

PENTECOST
The Church's birthday 25

BAPTISM
A new kind of bus ticket 26
Only one name 27
What's in a name? 28
Daddy 28

A YEAR OF SPECIAL DAYS

ST VALENTINE'S DAY
Valentine cards 33

LEAP YEAR
The Leap Year birthday 34

MOTHER'S DAY
You have only one mother 35
Mothers never go on strike 36

FATHER'S DAY
Special days 37

THE QUEEN'S BIRTHDAY
Trooping the Colour 38

AMERICAN INDEPENDENCE DAY
The freedom of Christ   39

HARVEST THANKSGIVING
Thorns   40
The harvest of happiness   41
Seeds or weeds?   41

HALLOWE'EN
False faces   43

REMEMBRANCE DAY
Remembrance   44
The computer   45

ST ANDREW'S DAY
The Saltire   46
Three people   47

ELECTION DAY
Choosing   48

CLOCK CHANGE DAY
No replays for us   49
The twenty-three hour day   50

THE SCHOOL YEAR

BEGINNING OF TERM
Back to school   53
Compensations   54
The first day at school   55

END OF TERM
The cattle show   56
The school report   57

SCHOOL HOLIDAYS

The passport	58
The perfume factory	59
The villagers of Eyam	60
The day of small things	61
Read the maker's instructions	62
Relations	63
Holiday weather	63

EVERYDAY THINGS

TRANSPORT

A road sign	67
Another road sign	67
Easter road signs	68
One-way streets	69
Kerb drill	70
L for Learner	70
Learning to drive	71
Seat-belts	72
Elephants	73
The bridge to God	74
The Transport Museum	75
Sundays only	75
Trains	76
Snow	77
"A1" at Lloyds	78
A walking stick	79

POWER

Telephones	80
The magic door	81
Sunlight	81
Organ pipes	82
The electric plug	83

Television   84
We need some power   85
The car key   86
God-made   87

SNEEZES AND WHEEZES
Your own temperature   88
The cold   89
The sneeze   89
The sore throat   90
The final certificate   91
It's infectious   92

GOD'S WONDERFUL WORLD
Something worth singing about   93
The greatest miracle of all   94
Window-boxes   95
Tree roots   95
The camel   96
The apple seed   98
Greedy monkey   98
Conkers   99
Honesty   100
The log of wood   101
The Bible Zoo   102
The Safari Park comes to town   103
The wasps' nest   104
The half horse   105
Crows   106
The Manse garden   106
More about the Manse garden
    (*Taraxacum Dens Leonis*)   107
The Manse garden again
    (*Sarcoptis*)   108

Pruning shears   109
Poor pelican   110
The bean that grew   111
The sweetpea chancel   112
The new planet   113
The mouse   114
The acorn   115

MONEY, TOKENS AND STAMPS
Children for sale   117
Millionaires   118
The communion token   -118
Blotting out the view   119
Stamps   120

TRACES LEFT BEHIND
The broken mirror   121
Fingerprints   121
A new suit   122
The vital clue   123
Confetti   124
The pawprint   125
The visiting card   126
Fair Isle pattern   127
Traces in the snow   128

CLOCKS, COMPASSES AND OTHER
   USEFUL THINGS
The King's clock   129
A luminous face   130
The Salisbury clock   131
The clock which tells lies   131
Seven days plus one   132
The clock which went backwards   133
The five minute clock   133

How to shorten sermons 135
Jesus the compass 135
Jesus is our measuring tape 136
The fault-finding chart 137
God's early-warning system 138
Reflections 138
The old lady and gentleman 139
Field glasses 140
Braille 141
Meters 141
The dictionary 142

CHRISTIAN LIFE

FORGIVENESS
Horrible Corner 147
Master Nobody 148
What's in my pocket? 149

PUTTING GOD FIRST
A scissor 150
First things first 151
Lessons 151
The ball that will not go straight 152
Single-minded 153
A place for everything 155

GOD'S LOVE FOR US
Through the night 156
The Get Better card 156
Greyfriars Bobby 157
A hint of gliding 158

USE YOUR BIBLE
Bibles are for reading 160

Don't keep it good!   160
The penknife   161
Pen-friends   162

WE ALL NEED EACH OTHER
Crazy arithmetic   164
The conductor   165
The missing glove   166
Together   167
The Pow-Wow   168
The Olympic logo   168
All together now!   169
Foreign languages   170
A three-fold cord   171
The hammer and the nail   172

LET US PRAY
The cannibal bus   174
Wait for an answer   175
Pray always   176
Perth and earth   176
Bedtime prayers   177
The God of patience   178
The Red Indian Princess   178
The boy who trusted   179
Stop talking   180
The tube of toothpaste   181
Prayers God doesn't answer   182
The hungry swans   182
Saint Bean   183
The ill shop   184

NO ONE HAS EVER SEEN GOD
The invisible God   186
The hidden God   187

Make a space for God   187
A mountain through a pin-hole   188
Parachutes   189

WHAT CAN LITTLE HANDS DO?
Put your whole self in   191
The Prime Minister   192
S.O.E.   192
The hands of Christ   193
Christ without hands   194
Glue, grit, jelly and soup   195
Spring cleaning   195
Lending a hand   196
John o' Groats house   197
Hearts need hands   198
D.I.Y.   199

BY THIS SHALL EVERYONE KNOW
The Battle Ensign   200
Badges   200
What is your tartan?   201
Liverymen of Christ   202

JESUS OUR MODEL
Carbon Paper   204
Funny faces   205
Liquorice Allsorts   205
My! How you've grown   206

A MISCELLANY
Swords into ploughshares   208
Give your heart to Jesus   209
Oh, for a plumber!   210
Jesus – the man for all men   210
Lost?   211

Take care of your feet, and your soul!   212
Nicknames   213
The boomerang   213
The favourite day   214
Be sincere   215
Blots   216
Chess   216
Books   217
Self-driven   218
The lost road   218
Don't be a dummy Christian   219
Salary   220
Think on these things   221
Seeking to save   222

THE CHURCH'S YEAR

CHRISTMAS

Jesus' birth certificate

What is this? £5 note.

What is this? A passport.

What is this? A birth certificate.

What is this? The most important birth certificate there's ever been – the story of the birth of Christ.

But for these few pages, you would have no holiday at Christmas, no presents, no cards, no church, no hope for poor lost mankind.

Mark you, Jesus' birth certificate won't matter to you unless Jesus matters to you.

Some people make a great fuss of Jesus' birthday and then forget about him for the other three hundred and sixty-four days of the year. That won't do. One of the worst crimes in the world is to neglect a baby, and many of us do that to the baby Jesus. We fuss over him for one day and then forget all about him. It is as if your mother gave you a lovely birthday and then forgot to give you any food for all ther rest of the year.

We can enjoy Jesus' birthday only if we learn to know Jesus as our friend and obey him as our Lord. Only then can it matter to us that this was how the birth of Jesus took place.

———————— · ————————

Will Jesus be here?

I was in Edinburgh the other day and went into a big shop in Princes Street to buy something. As I was leaving, a lady was coming in with her little boy. The boy asked his mother a question. I couldn't quite hear what it was, but I heard his mother's reply. She said, "No, he *won't* be here. He only comes at Christmas time." Who was it the little boy hoped to see? Santa Claus, of course. But he'd have to wait a long time, for Santa Claus only appears at Christmas.

Some people think that Jesus is like that too – that he only comes at Christmas, or perhaps only at Christmas and Easter. But that's not true. He once sid, "Where two or three are gathered together in my name, I am there with them." So he's here today, though we can't see him.

If the same little boy going into church this morning asks, "Will Jesus be here?", the answer is, "Yes, he's here every Sunday," and not only here, but everywhere; and not only every Sunday, but every day and all day, whether we know it or not.

For he once said, "I will be with you always, even to the end of the world." *(Matthew 28.20)*

_____ · _____

The first chapter

I wonder what presents you will be given on Christmas Day, boys and girls? There will be something from your father and mother, and maybe from your grandparents; and, of course, there's always Santa Claus. You can rely on him. He never lets a good boy or girl down.

Among your presents, most of you will be given at least one book – a nice, clean, shiny, new book. That's one of the best presents, for it lasts such a long time.

But if you do get a book, be sure to read it all. There would be no sense in reading the first chapter and then laying it aside. You've got to read all of it to discover what happens.

The story of Christmas is a wonderful story, but it is only the very first chapter of a long story – a story which is still being written.

Christmas is just the first chapter of the story of Jesus and his love, his words and his death – a story which still goes on, for Christ is still at work to make his world a better, happier place; still at work to make us better boys and girls and men and women.

So don't be content with the first chapter of Christ's life written in Bethlehem.

Go on to read all about him in the New Testament and about the history of his Church, right up to the present day.

——————— · ———————

Bicycle or tricycle?

Are you looking forward to Christmas? I'm sure you are. I am. A boy I know, called David, was really looking forward to Christmas, for he very much wanted a bike. Indeed, every night at the end of his prayers, he said, "Please God, let me have a bike for Christmas." Maybe he hoped that his father and mother were listening, as well as God.

David was a very young boy, and his mother and father thought it wouldn't be safe for him to have a bike, so they bought him a tricycle instead. When Christmas came, there was the tricycle waiting for him when he got up. It was a very nice tricycle and David was a polite little boy, so he said, "Thank you very much." His father said, "I hope you're pleased with your tricycle, David?", to which David replied, "Yes, but you'd think God would know the difference between a bike and a trike!"

Well, God knows the difference between a bike and a trike. God knew how much David wanted a bike, but he also knew what was best for him. Maybe David will get a real bike some day soon, but not yet.

God is always polite. He always answers our prayers. Often he says, "Yes." Sometimes he says "No." Occasionally he says "Later, but not yet." But he always answers and he never refuses us anything that is for our good. The proof of this is that he did not even refuse to give his son to be the friend and saviour of us all.

——————— · ———————

The most important Christmas card

Well, boys and girls, have you got all your Christmas cards written and posted? If you haven't, I'm afraid you're too late for posting. You'll have to deliver them by hand now.

It is terrible on Christmas Eve suddenly to remember somebody you've forgotten – somebody you should have remembered, who has perhaps sent you a card. Yet, of course, you can't send a Christmas card to everybody you know.

Only *one* person ever did that. He sent a Christmas greeting to everybody in the world. You know who that was – God himself. For, if you think of it, all a Christmas card does is to wish you joy at Christmas and tell you of the love of the person who sent it.

And God's Christmas greeting does just that. You'll find it in the second chapter of St. Luke's gospel. "I bring you glad tidings of great joy, which shall be to all people."

We may forget someone at Christmas time, but God forgets nobody. He sends his message of love to all people everywhere – and to you and to me.

——————— · ———————

Christmas post

Girls and boys, did you enjoy your Sunday School party yesterday? You were only at one. I was at three and Santa Claus turned up, as cheery as you like, at every one. He's a wonderful chap is Santa Claus.

Almost as wonderful as Santa Claus is someone else – the postman or postwoman. If you think of all the millions and millions of letters and parcels and Christmas cards which are sent from all over the world, it is wonderful that they all reach the right person. Well – nearly all.

The other day I got a very large, interesting-looking letter with a foreign stamp on it. I picked up a letter opener and was just on the point of cutting open the envelope when suddenly I noticed that for once the Post Office had made a mistake. The letter was not for me at all, but for somebody else in the town with the same name.

We should always be careful before we open a parcel or letter and make sure that it is really meant for us and not for the person next door, or for someone across the street, or for someone with a name like ours.

Well, boys and girls, there is one Christmas present – and that is the first and the best – which *is* for you, for all of you, for it is labelled clearly in God's own hand; and the present is the gift of God's own son to be the saviour and the friend of us all.

The Angel said that the good news was to be given "to all people", and, in case there should be any doubt, went on to say, "unto *you* is born a saviour, which is Christ the Lord."

That is why we must always go on trying to make sure that everybody – black people and white, Chinese and Indian, African and Russian – that everybody hears and knows of this, the best Christmas present in the world – Christ born to be their saviour.

There is no mistake about this present. It is "to all" and "to you."

Find the baby

One of those very cold days, a strange thing came to our house. It was a bundle of clothes; at least that is what it looked like. So we began to take it apart. First of all there was a waterproof. Underneath that there was a woolly coat. There was a beret too and a scarf and one or two cardigans and a pair of long trousers. Underneath everything, quite hidden by all the clothes, was a little boy.

Christmas is a bit like that. It comes to us, all wrapped up in so many things – crackers and presents and turkey and holly, Christmas cards and Christmas pies. All very nice wrappings, but only the wrappings.

What matters at Christmas time is that little boy – sometimes quite hidden under the wrappings – the little boy Jesus, who came to this world to be the friend of us all.

It is up to us to "find the baby."

——————— · ———————

The first Christmas present

Why did you bring presents to this Christmas Gift Service? Perhaps you're not very sure. Well, let me tell you.

Sometimes at Christmas a terrible thing happens. Someone gives us a present and we have forgotten to buy a present for them.

Well, there is one present which every one of us will receive, the first Christmas present that was ever given, and it has been given again every Christmas since. For on the first Christmas Day, God gave his love to all men by sending his son into the world, and on this Christmas Day he will give that love again. What can we give him in return? It is hard to give presents to grown-ups, for often they seem to have everything. God surely has everything he wants.

But he hasn't, you know. There is one present God wants at Christmas, a present only you can give – the love and obedience of your hearts.

But how can we show God that we love him and want to obey him? He has told us that too. Once Jesus said, "Whenever you did this for one of the least important of these brothers of mine, you did it for me."

Chocolates

I don't know how it is in your house, but when there is a box of chocolates in the Manse, before I even know that the box has been opened, all the nice hard-centres I like seem to have disappeared. The only ones left are the violet creams and the Brazil nuts, which I don't care for.

But the other day I was alone in the Manse when a parcel came, all wrapped up in Christmassy paper. It looked as if it might be a box of chocolates. Now I know as well as you do that one is not supposed to open Christmas parcels till Christmas Day, but I was tempted. I thought to myself, "If I open the box and eat one or two of the ones I really like, when the others come in they may be cross but there will be nothing they can do about it." I was just on the point of yielding to temptation and ripping open the paper when I looked at the label. Horror of horrors – the parcel wasn't for us at all. It was just someone using the Manse as a post office in the hope of saving a few pence. How awful it would have been if I had opened it! What would the person it was addressed to have thought when she asked for it?

Anybody who is thinking of leaving a parcel at the Manse for someone else had better write the name and address in nice big letters, just in case I'm tempted again and don't look too closely.

We should all be very careful before we open a parcel or a letter, and make sure that it is really meant for us and not for the lady next door or down the street.

Well, girls and boys, there is one Christmas present which you will each receive – the first and the best – and this present is especially for you.

_____ · _____

NEW YEAR

Just one more present

Have you had all the presents you want? Would you like just one more? Tomorrow morning you'll have one – the present of a nice, bright, shiny, New Year – just like one of those lovely books you got from Santa Claus which had never been opened – clean and fresh. We should not soil nor waste any of the presents we're given, but least of all this present of a New Year. Let's not spoil it with blots of bad temper or lies or cruelty.

And, since we've been given a present, we should give one in return. Since God has given us life and the present of a New Year, let us give him the New Year present he wants – our love and our obedience day by day.

That is what St. Paul meant when he said, "Offer yourselves as a living sacrifice to God, dedicated to his service and pleasing to him." *(Romans 12.1)*

--- · ---

The diary

How do you like my new diary, boys and girls? It is a present from a friend who gives me one every year. Here is last year's one, all tatty and used. At midnight on New Year's Eve I'll throw it out and start on the nice, new, fresh one.

At midnight on that night, we'll all get a present from another friend – the present of a nice, clean, fresh, New Year. Then we'll put out the Old Year – all tatty and spoiled. With it, let's put out

11

our old bad habits, temper, selfishness, laziness and lies, and start afresh and, with the help of God who gives it to us, make it a happy, good, New Year for ourselves and for everybody we'll meet in it. We can, you know, for God said, "I make all things new." *(Revelation 21.5)*

Visitors

Girls and boys, I hope that you had a very Happy Christmas and that you are having a good New Year. One of the nice things about this season of the year is that it is a great time for visitors, and visitors are usually fun. You never get a row when strangers are in the house (at least I don't!), and usually you get something special to eat. Parents are always on their best behaviour when there are visitors around. It is especially nice when visitors come and stay for a few days – people like grandparents.

A stranger came to a home in Dunblane last year who is going to stay for years and years. Next Baptismal Sunday, a father and mother to whom such a stranger came will bring him to the Cathedral to meet us all. You know who the stranger is – a baby.

A visitor who came to all our homes at Christmas time was Christ. He is hoping that, now that his birthday is past, we won't put him out into the cold. He's hoping we'll ask him to stay. If we do, he will stay with us, not just for one meal, nor for a few days, but for ever and ever. That is what he promised to do. He once said, "I will be with you always, even to the end," and Christ always keeps his promise.

The good companion

Just after Christmas I met a boy I know, standing idly around near his home. I asked him, "Are you going somewhere?" and he said, "Yes." But when I asked him where he was going, he said "I don't know." I teased him a little and told him he wouldn't get very far if he didn't know where he was going. But he got the last word. He said, "I may not know where I'm going, but I'm going with my friend." And that made me think.

Here we are on the first Sunday of this year. As we look forward into the New Year, we really do not know where we are going, nor what is going to happen to us at school, or on the sports field, or at home. Most of us don't know where we will be going for our holidays. For some of us there may be big changes ahead. We don't know where we are going, but this we do know, that wherever we go and whatever happens to us, we can have Christ with us as our Friend in every day of the year and beyond that for ever. That is all that really matters.

Jesus said, "I am with you alway, even unto the end." *(Matthew 28.20)*

The new calendar

I hope you've got a nice new calendar, boys and girls. It's pretty important to have at least one calendar in every house. After all, without a calendar we could easily miss Christmas, or New Year, or our birthdays, or even our holidays, and that would never do. Imagine waking up one day to discover that Christmas was over and we'd never noticed!

The kind of calendar I like best is the kind with a new leaf for every week. Every Monday I turn over a new page and there's a nice clean sheet saying, "A good new week to you, Mr. Gray." I always think – now I'm going to do much better this week than I did last week. The calendar I like best of all is the one which has a different picture for every week in the year. There isn't time to grow tired of one picture before turning the page to a fresh one.

It would be rather nice if *we* could do that, if you and I could have a new look every week and decide to be tall one week and short the next, dark one week and fair, or redhaired, the next.

Well, we can't and that's that. We can't even have a new face once a year. We must just learn to put up with the old one all our lives. Anyway, it does not much matter what we look like – what does matter is what we *are* like; and although faces can't be changed, we can. We need not go on being the same selfish, bad-tempered people we've always been. We won't be if we ask Jesus to take charge of our lives.

If we do, this will be a really and truly Happy New Year, not only for ourselves, but for all who know us.

———————— · ————————

EPIPHANY

The Wise Men

This is the Sunday when we remember the Wise Men who came to search for Jesus when he was little. When they found him, they offered him three gifts. What were these gifts? Gold, frankincense and myrrh – all very precious things. Have you ever wondered what makes something precious? Why is gold more precious than coal? Why is frankincense more precious than water and myrrh more precious than margarine? A thing is precious when it is scarce – when there's not much of it. There is far more coal in the world than gold, far more water than frankincense, and far more margarine than myrrh. It was because the three things they brought were very scarce, and therefore very precious, that the Wise Men offered them to Jesus.

God has been very good to us, giving us life in this wonderful world, loving parents, a comfortable home and all the fun of Christmas. It would be wonderful if you and I could offer God a present, something very scarce and very precious. The most precious thing in the world would be something of which there was only one in all the world. Such things we call unique. Would it not be wonderful if you and I had something unique that we could offer to God, best of all if it were something he wanted very much? Well, we have just that.

There's only one of you and only one of me. You and I are unique and so we are each very precious. That is the gift God wants more than anything else – just that we should, each of us, give him the love of our hearts and our obedience day by day.

———————— · ————————

Gold, frankincense and myrrh

Well, girls and boys, Christmas is over for another year and there will be no more Christmas presents for fifty whole weeks. But Christmas is not the only time when we give presents to each other, is it? I'm sure you all get presents on your birthday, and people who are getting married usually get lots of presents from friends and relations.

There is another time when we often give a present – when a baby is born. Last Tuesday was Epiphany. That's the day we remember some people who gave presents to Jesus when he was a baby. Who were they? They were, of course, the Wise Men who came from the East. What were the presents they gave? I'm sure you know that too. They were gold, frankincense and myrrh. I like to give every new baby a present when I baptise him or her. I can't afford to give gold and I don't know where I would find frankincense or myrrh, but I give the baby something far more valuable than all the gold and frankincense in the world. I give a little book, the New Testament, in which, when they grow up, the babies may learn how much God loves them, and how he came into the world to be the friend and saviour of us all.

THE FLIGHT INTO EGYPT

The Spider

Today I'm going to tell you a story. I don't know if it is true or not, but it is very old. It is about the time when Jesus, still a baby, was being taken by his father and mother to Egypt to escape cruel King Herod. One cold night they hid in a cave. In the cave there was a little spider. The spider was very sorry for the baby and wondered what it could do to help. There wasn't much, but it thought to itself, "If I spin my web across the door of the cave, it will keep some of the cold out," and that is just what it did. When Herod's soldiers came, they looked at the spider's web, all covered with frost, and said, "Well, there's nobody in there or they'd have broken the spider's web," and so Jesus and his father and mother were kept safe.

That is why every year at Christmas time, in memory of the little spider and its frost-covered web, we put tinsel on the Christmas tree.

I don't know if the story is true, but it is worth telling, for it reminds us that God can use our gifts, however small or unimportant, as long as we offer them gladly and lovingly to him, like the Wise Men who offered Christ their gifts.

———————— · ————————

PALM SUNDAY

Palms

This is Palm Sunday – called that because on this day Jesus, our Lord, entered Jerusalem, and was welcomed by children crying, "Hosanna to the Son of David." To show how welcome he was, some of them took branches of palms and waved them like flags or spread them before Jesus' feet.

Well, that all happened a long time ago. Palms, such as the children of Jerusalem had, don't grow in Scotland. But there is one kind of palm that we all have – the palms of our hands, and we can show Christ how much we love him by using these palms properly.

We can please Christ by the *work* we do with our palms for other people – chopping wood, washing dishes, doing shopping – for whenever we help other people, we help him.

We can please Christ by the *gifts* that we make – by what we give to other people and to his church.

We can also please Christ by *holding up our hands* in loyalty to him. Once in school I asked who had been at church last Sunday and not a single soul held up his or her hand. I knew some had been there, but they were too shy.

But it helps Christ if, when anybody speaks of him, you and I put up our hands and show our loyalty to him.

These are the palms which really please Jesus – the willing palm of service, the open palm of generosity, the raised palm of loyalty.

——————— · ———————

By appointment   St J 1993.

I think I know what the Queen had for breakfast today. At least, on one side of this packet of Corn Flakes is the Coat of Arms of the Queen and it says, "By appointment to Queen Elizabeth II." Mark you, I believe they're on Rice Krispies and Porridge Oats too. Perhaps the Queen has a different cereal every day of the week, just to keep everybody happy. The only people who can write "By appointment" on their packets and print the Royal Coat of Arms are those who have supplied their goods to the Queen.

Today is Palm Sunday – the day when we remember that our Lord Jesus Christ rode into Jerusalem to die, on a donkey. If you look at any donkey's back, you'll see a cross quite clearly marked on it, the mark of the King who was humble enough to ride upon it. "By appointment to King Jesus", the donkey bears his royal sign and should be honoured for the service that once it gave to the King of Kings.

When babies are baptised, they are sprinkled with water as proof that they have been appointed to serve the Great King. You and I were all baptised once and so we should be proud to be of use to him who said of a little donkey, "The Master needs him." (Luke 19.31)

——————— · ———————

EASTER

StJ

The cross which endures

A long time ago, during the last war, I was a chaplain, that is, a sort of minister, in the Royal Navy. For a while I was at a place called Scapa Flow – away in the North, almost as far as you can go. Every Sunday evening at nine o'clock, I held a service in the Chapel of a big battleship called *H.M.S. King George V*. On the communion table in the Chapel there was a simple wooden cross which the ship's carpenter had made.

After the war was over, I heard that *H.M.S. King George V* was being broken up in Clydebank, a town on the Clyde, near Glasgow. One day I went down to see what was left of the great ship. I asked the man in charge if I could see the Chapel. He said I could, although they had already started to break it up. It was in a dreadful mess, but in a corner I saw the little wooden cross. I asked if I could have it to keep and the foreman said, "Of course," and now it stands in my study, on my desk.

The great battleship with its fourteen-inch guns has all disappeared – made into razor blades or Coca-Cola tins. All that is left of it is the wooden cross.

When Jesus died, people thought that that was the end of him, that everyone would soon forget the man on the cross. But it is the people who hated Christ who have been forgotten and the cross which is remembered, for it tells of the love of God for us all – love that was finally stronger than death itself.

St-J

To be continued

What programme do you like best on television? Maybe you like them all. The only bit you don't like, perhaps, is when they come to an end. For whenever all the names of the producers and actors start coming up the screen at the end of the programme, there's sure to be a grown-up on hand to say, "Right, off to bed now," or, "Put that thing off and get on with your homework."

One boy I know says his favourite programmes are serials, the kind where the story carries on from week to week. He likes them best because as he goes off to bed, or gets out his school books, he cheers himself up by thinking, "Oh well, there will be another instalment next week."

The most wonderful story in the world is the story of Jesus who came into the world to heal and help. That story seemed to have come to an end, to a dead stop, when Jesus was crucified.

The reason we are so glad at Easter is because we now know that it was not "The End" – the story of Jesus has been continued. He is still in the world, helping men and women, boys and girls, to live brave and good and kindly lives. Though he died so long ago, Jesus lives.

And because he lives, we shall live also. Our lives seem to come to an end when we die and are buried. But it is not so. Our lives are "to be continued" on the other side of death. That is the message of Easter.

So don't be afraid of anything in life and don't be afraid even of death. It is not the end of life. It is only the end of one episode in a story which will be continued for ever. As Jesus told us, "Because I live, you shall live also." *(John 14.19)*

StJ

The end

What kind of stories do you like, boys and girls? Westerns perhaps, stories like Wells Fargo or Wyatt Earp or the Lone Ranger, or fairy stories about Cinderella or Tinkerbell? Or maybe you like stories like *Masterman Ready* or *Captain Courageous*, or stories about people like *Little Women* or *Heidi*, or those about birds and animals? Perhaps you like them all – except the cruel, silly ones of course. There is no use reading books which make you unhappy or afraid. But every book, no matter how good it is, has two words in it which make girls and boys at least a little miserable, especially at bedtime. You know what those two words are. They are always on the last page. Yes! They are "The End."

Long ago the Lord Jesus was cruelly killed, and his friends were sad, because they all thought that it was "The End". Why we are so glad on Easter Sunday is because we know now that it was not the end. It was not much more than the beginning of a wonderful, continued story which shall never end – the story of God's love and power. Everything else comes to an end. It is this which causes most of the sadness in the world. Every story however beautiful, every life however long has its end; every empire, every kingdom shall pass away except that of Christ. But he has faced death and conquered it and so, "of his Kingdom there shall be no end." *(Luke 1.33)*

Nobody Knows What

Do you know where New Zealand is, boys and girls? Right on the other side of the world. One of the first British sailors to visit New Zealand was Captain Cook, who named many of the bays and towns in New Zealand. He didn't give them ordinary names like Dunblane or Glasgow, but thought of some very entertaining names, like Bay of Plenty, Pleasant Point, Doubtful Sound, Hen and Chicken Islands. But Captain Cook did not reach the whole of New Zealand. There was one bay he couldn't reach at all, and so he gave it a very funny name indeed – he called it "Nobody Knows What."

Twenty years after Captain Cook, another sailor called Captain Vancouver went to New Zealand and finished Captain Cook's work. When he came to the bay called "Nobody Knows What", he gave it a new name. He called it "*Somebody* Knows What."

Before Jesus came, people were very afraid of death. If they spoke about it at all, they would say that nobody knows what lies beyond. But why *we* are happy at Easter is because Jesus has died, and has risen, and has told us that none of us need be afraid of what lies beyond. Now we know that somebody – Jesus – knows what lies beyond.

The Ascension

Girls and boys, which direction is east? Which direction is west? Which is north and which is south? Many churches were built from west to east so that when the people in the congregation were worshipping, they were facing east towards where Bethlehem is, the place where Jesus was born, and Jerusalem, where he died and rose, and from where he returned to his Father's side.

Of course Jesus is not there any more, nor is he up in the sky among the clouds. We know that he is with God and that those who loved him and are no longer here are with him. That surely is enough without our knowing exactly where they are. We talk about going "up to Aberdeen", or "down to London", but Aberdeen's not up there nor London down there.

That is why after Jesus disappeared, the disciples were asked "Why do you stand looking up?" In Jesus there is no east or west, no north or south, no up or down. He is wherever and whenever we need him. *(Acts 1.11)*

——————— · ———————

PENTECOST

The Church's birthday

I'm glad to see you, boys and girls, for today is a special day – it is a birthday. It is not mine and it probably isn't any of yours either. It is a one thousand, nine hundred and fifty-third birthday, and you're not one thousand, nine hundred and fifty-three – and neither am I.

Today is the birthday of the Church. This is Whitsunday or Pentecost – the day on which we remember how God gave life to the Church by sending his Holy Spirit.

The Church is different from us, she gets older, but she gets younger every day too. For God, if we ask him to, keeps sending his Holy Spirit into the Church and into our hearts and lives, to fill us with new life.

———————— · ————————

BAPTISM

A new kind of bus ticket

Do you ever lose tickets, boys and girls? I'm forever losing them, especially on the bus or the train. When the Inspector comes along, I say, "I had one, I know, " and then I search all my pockets and have a look on the floor, while my face gets redder and redder and the Inspector gets angrier and angrier.

In America, in some places, especially sports arenas, they have a good idea. Instead of giving you a silly bit of cardboard or paper, they stamp the back of your hand with a rubber stamp covered with invisible ink. You can see nothing unless you put your hand under a special lamp and then the day and the date and the price you've paid can all be read quite easily. Perhaps the bus company and British Rail will get around to it some time. It would save a lot of trouble and a lot of litter if they would. Though you can't see the mark, it is always there.

Today we're going to baptise some babies. After they've been baptised, they'll look just the same as before. Yet for ever after they will bear the mark of Christ invisibly upon them and belong to his family on earth, which is the Church. Of course, when they grow up they'll have to make up their own minds and I hope they'll decide, and you will too, to follow Christ and to obey his commands.

If we've done that, it cannot be hidden. It will show by the fact that we are honest and truthful, cheerful, brave and kind.

Jesus said, "If you obey my teaching, you are really my disciples." *(John 8.31)*

———————— · ————————

Only one name

Do you know what a slave is, girls and boys? It is a person who can't do what he or she likes, nor go where he or she wants. Slaves have to work for their masters and get no pay for it – just the poorest of food and clothes and shelter. Well, happily there aren't many slaves left in the world, but there used to be millions.

Once in America I met a very old black gentleman whose grandfather had been a slave and he had been bought and sold just like a horse or a cow. He told me something I hadn't known before about slaves – they had only one name. You and I have two or more names. Our last name, or surname, is the same as our mother's and father's and brothers' and sisters'. Our first names are called our Christian names, because they are given to us when we are christened or baptised. But in the bad old days the slaves had no surnames like Smith or Jones or Gray and the only name they each had was their Christian name – the one they had been given when they were baptised. They were known simply as Samuel or John or Mary. There's something wonderful in that. However little people cared for the slaves, God cared and knew each by his or her own name.

You all know your names, of course. Everybody in Church knows his or her own name. But in a short while we'll have two people in Church who don't know their names. I'll call them by their Christian names, but they won't answer. Who will they be? The babies. It will be a very long time before David and Karen know their own names or answer when they're called, but that doesn't matter, for God knows them by name. He has known them from the very beginning and has loved each of them as he loves each one of us and always will.

God once said, "I have called you by name. You are mine." *(Isaiah 43.1)*

What's in a name?

A lady came up to me this week and said, "My, you are looking well, and how young! It must be twenty years since we met and you haven't changed a bit." I would have been very pleased, except that I had no idea who the lady was and had never seen her before in my life. I must have looked a bit doubtful, for she went on to say, "Do you remember me, Mr. Anderson?"

Well, I've nothing against Anderson as a name, except that it's not mine. Gray may not be a very fancy name, but I've had it for a long time and I've got used to it and I'll just stick to it.

All the same, only yesterday afternoon someone came into church with one name, and I took a short service and the person left the church very happy with a new name. What kind of service was it that changed the person's name?

Of course, only the bride's second name, her surname, had changed. She kept the Christian name she's always had.

Later on in this service, I shall be baptising a little baby. Before doing so, I shall call her by name, and that name, her Christian name, she will have all her life. It is by that name that God will know her always, just as he knows each one of us – by our own name.

How God manages to know every one of the millions of people in the world, I can't tell, but he does.

Jesus has told us that we should call God "Father", and like any father, God knows and loves each one of his children, just as if there were no other to love.

———————— · ————————

Daddy

You know, boys and girls, that I often go to see people who are in hospital. A while ago I was in a children's ward where sick boys and girls are made well. No sooner had I walked into the ward than a little girl, not much more than a baby, in a cot at the far end, became very excited and began to shout, "Daddy, Daddy, Daddy." So I walked up the ward to talk to her and she kept on saying, "Daddy, Daddy." Then suddenly, when she saw me clearly, she said, "Man," and lay down and turned her head away.

She wasn't much more than a year old, so it was very clever of her to see that I wasn't her daddy, but only – a man. For at first, of course, babies don't know their own fathers. One man seems just the same as another to them.

But, no matter how little babies are, even though they don't know their fathers, their fathers always know them.

This morning, some babies are going to be baptised. These babies don't know anything about God, their heavenly father. But God knows each of them and is ready to show by sprinkled water that he loves each one and wants each one to be his own child for ever.

A YEAR OF SPECIAL DAYS

ST VALENTINE'S DAY

Valentine cards

Yesterday I was given something which I really should not have been given until Friday. What's special about Friday? If I tell you it's February 14th, does that help? If I show you what I was given, does that help? It's not a Christmas card. It's not a Birthday card. It's a Valentine.

Well, I didn't get my Valentine from a girl, but from a boy, and it's a bit second-hand too, but I'm hoping that I'll get some more on Friday.

It is very nice to be told that somebody loves you, but we shouldn't just say "I love you" on February 14th. We should say it often to the people whom we love.

Even God likes to be told that we love him. That is what we do when we sing our hymns and say our prayers. But we shouldn't only say it. We should show it.

As Jesus said, "He who knows my commandments and does them, he it is who loves me." *(John 14.21)*

———————— · ————————

LEAP YEAR

The Leap Year birthday

I have a friend, girls and boys, who has only had seventeen birthdays. What day is his birthday? February 29th. That means he has a birthday only every four years. What age is he? Seventeen times four.

Well, it is bad enough to wait a whole year for a birthday, but he has to wait four years. At least, he should, but he doesn't, for although his children are grown up, they haven't forgotten their father, and every year on February 28th, even though it is not his birthday, they send him cards and presents.

Actually, none of us needs to wait for a birthday to be generous and kind to people or to show people that we love them and tell them so.

There's nothing to stop you going home and saying to your parents, "As it's *not* your birthday, I want to tell you how much I love you" – you try it.

Certainly, God does not wait for any special day to show his love for us. Always and everywhere, in a thousand ways, he shows us how much he cares for us.

In Leap Years, in ordinary years, on Sundays, on weekdays, in winter and summer, when we're young and when we're old, God loves each of us just as if there were no-one else to love, and he will love us like that for ever. He once said, "I have loved you with an everlasting love" – that means with a love which never grows tired and never changes and never ends.

That is the good news Christ came into the world to tell us all.

———————— · ————————

MOTHER'S DAY

You have only one mother

Have you ever noticed that you get two of some things and only one of others? You get two eyes and two ears, but only one mouth. It seems you're meant to do twice as much listening and looking as talking. You get two arms and two legs, so you're meant to do twice as much working and walking as sitting around.

That is one reason why we should be very good to our mothers, for each of us has only one; which brings me to the fact that today is Mother's Day. At least, that is what my diary says, but someone on the radio yesterday said that Mother's Day is really the second Sunday in May. It is really very confusing to have two Mother's Days, but only one mother.

The best thing would be to let every day be Mother's Day. After all, your mother is good and kind and comforting to you every day in the year. And Isaiah tells us that is what God is like.

"I will comfort you as a mother comforts a child," said the Lord. It's a lovely word, comfort. Do you know what it really means? It means to make strong. So we don't need to be ashamed of being comforted by our mothers or by God. It is not a sign of weakness, but the secret of strength.

"I will comfort you as a mother comforts her child," said the Lord. *(Isaiah 66.13)*

Mothers never go on strike

Boys and girls, do you know what a strike is? It is when people refuse to work.

Now, who works very hard, for long hours, every day in the week, for most weeks in the year, is never paid and never goes on strike?

There are about one thousand mothers in our town, doing nearly all the housework and cleaning and washing and bed-making and shopping and cooking and baking. There are nearly a million mothers in Scotland and about five hundred million mothers in the world, all working away without any payment – without any payment in money, that is. But they would say that they are paid. What are they paid with? Love.

This is Mother's Day. Even if you have forgotten to buy your mother a present, she won't mind if you tell her how much you love her – and you should tell her, not only today, but every day.

There is someone else who never goes on strike and is never paid, except with love, and that is God. He has the biggest family anybody could have – all the men and women and boys and girls in the world – and he loves each one just as if he had nobody else to love.

We should repay God too for all his goodness, with our love, and not just today because it is Sunday, the Lord's Day, but every day.

FATHER'S DAY

Special days

Today is Father's Day, girls and boys. Some people don't think much of having a special day set aside for us to remember father. I'm rather in favour of it – I got some chocolate gingers this morning, first thing.

We could have more of it. We could have a Son's Day and a Daughter's Day and a Brother's and Sister's Day and an Auntie's and an Uncle's Day and a Grandpa's and a Grannie's Day, a Neighbour's Day and a School Friend's Day and a Doctor's Day and a Teacher's Day and a Dustman's Day – days on which we'd remember to be thankful for all the people who help us and do us good. It's a good idea, so long as we do not forget or neglect these people every other day in the year.

One of the other names for Sunday is "The Lord's Day". That's a fine name, just so long as it does not make us think that only one day in the week belongs to God. By all means let us remember father on Father's Day, but not only then. By all means let us remember God on the first day of the week, but not only then.

Jesus said, "If anyone wants to come with me he must . . . take up his cross every day, and follow me." *(Luke 9.23)*

THE QUEEN'S BIRTHDAY

Trooping the Colour

How many birthdays do you have each year? Just one. There is only one person I know who has two birthdays. She had a birthday yesterday, her second birthday this year. Who is it? The Queen. Yesterday was her official birthday and she had an odd sort of party for it. Maybe you saw it on television? It was called "Trooping the Colour". What happened was that the Colour – the flag – of one of the regiments of Guards was carried up and down in front of the Queen and in front of all the soldiers who were there.

Now it is just a splendid sort of parade, but once it was very important that every soldier should know his own flag and so know where to go in the middle of the battle.

Every Sunday is a kind of Trooping the Colour for those who call Jesus Lord. Every Sunday we come to church to learn to know Jesus a little better, so that, no matter what difficulties we may have to face, we may stay close to him. If we do we will never have to be afraid, and we will know what to answer when we hear the question, "Who is on the Lord's side?"

———————— · ————————

AMERICAN INDEPENDENCE DAY

The freedom of Christ

At the end of the service today, we're going to sing a hymn called "The Battle Hymn of the Republic." The first line is "Mine eyes have seen the glory of the coming of the Lord." The Americans look on this hymn in much the same way as we look on "God Save the Queen."

Why are we going to sing it today? This is American Independence Day. On July 4th, people in America remember the time, about two hundred years ago, long before the hymn was written, when their ancestors fought for and finally obtained their independence from Britain, when they threw off what they felt to be a tyranny. Who was their great leader? George Washington.

Today we are glad with our American friends in the freedom in which they live.

Two thousand years ago a far greater leader than George Washington was born into the world, Jesus, our Lord. He came, not to set one nation free, but so that all people everywhere might be free from falsehood and wrong and cruelty and injustice.

Real freedom is not "doing what you like." It is doing what you ought to do, and liking it. Christ will help us to do that. If our lives are spent in his service, we shall be free, free from two tyrants, selfishness and sin.

As St. Paul once said, "Christ has set us free." *(Galatians 5.1)*

——————— · ———————

HARVEST THANKSGIVING

Thorns

In my left hand, girls and boys, I have a little glass dish with some delicious fruit in it. I didn't buy the fruit. It was not given to me. I didn't steal it from the Harvest Thanksgiving gifts. It could be eaten just as it is with ice-cream. It could be made into the filling for a tart or it could be made into jelly.

In my right hand I have nothing but a few purple stains and some scratches.

What kind of fruit is it? Brambles, of course.

It is great fun brambling. I'll tell you some good places to go this afternoon. But no matter where you go and how careful you may be, you won't gather brambles without being scratched by the thorns. That's the price you pay for the brambles.

If you think of it, these lovely fruits and flowers and vegetables all cost something. They didn't just grow. The gardeners had to dig and sow and weed and water for months.

That is why these gifts are worth giving to God, because they cost something in effort and pain and sacrifice. That is the only way in which you get good results in a garden or in life.

A boy I know was looking at the organ yesterday and said he'd like to be able to play it. So he will one day, but before that day comes, there will have to be hours and hours of hard practice.

The same is true of learning to ski or to play golf, to be a nurse or a teacher or even a minister. You've got to be ready for hard work and self-sacrifice if you are going to do anything worth-while in life.

It is certainly true of learning to be a Christian. Jesus once said, "If any one will come after me, let him deny himself and take up his cross daily and follow me." *(Luke 9.23)*

The harvest of happiness

Grown-ups sometimes do very strange things. Every spring and autumn, some friends of mine do something very odd. They go into town, pay a great deal of money for something, and when they get home with it, do you know what they do? They throw it down on the ground and cover it up with earth! You wouldn't spend your money on something and then bury it in the ground, would you?

It seems a silly thing to do, but farmers are not a bit silly and that is just what they do. Every spring and autumn they pay lots of money for something and they take it home to throw on the ground. What is it? Seed, of course. If the farmers didn't buy seed and put it in the ground, there would be no harvest and nothing for any of us to eat. If the farmer said, "I'm not going to buy expensive seed and put it in the ground. I'm going to keep it in my house," he wouldn't be any richer. He would soon be very poor indeed and we would be very hungry.

That is true of other things too. If you want to reap a harvest of happiness, you've got to try to give happiness away, to make others happy – the more happiness you give away, the happier you'll be yourself.

This is true of your whole life. If you try to live for yourself, your life will become poorer all the time. Only if you use your life for other people will you find what fun life can be.

Jesus once said, "Whoever tries to gain his own life will lose it; but whoever loses his life for my sake will gain it." *(Matthew 10.39)*

———————— · ————————

Seeds or weeds?

Do you know what this is? It's the seed from an ear of oats. If you plant it in the ground, it will grow until from this one seed will come another ear of oats with lots of seed on it.

Do you know what this is? It's the seed of a weed which could grow up and choke all the oats it's growing among.

If you were a farmer, what would you plant? Every time you come to church or Sunday School, every time you pray, every time you read or listen to the Bible, God is planting a good seed in your heart and life.

Every time you tell a lie, every time you steal, every time you listen to things you shouldn't listen to, you're planting a bad seed in your heart and life.

Let Jesus into your hearts and into your lives and he'll plant so many seeds that there won't even be the least little bit of room left for all the wicked and cruel things to grow.

———————— · ————————

HALLOWE'EN

False faces

I hope you are going to have lots of fun at Hallowe'en, and that you will do some dressing up and will have a false face – a nice hideous one with a great big hooked nose and a few ugly teeth. It is fun to put on a false face at Hallowe'en, when everybody knows it is a false face. But not all the time. It would be horrid to wear a false face all the time. Yet some people do. They pretend to be what they are not and not to be what they are. They say nice things to people to their faces and nasty things behind their backs. They pretend to be friendly and kind, but underneath they're just as mean and nasty as can be.

People like that made Jesus very angry. He called such people "hypocrites" and once he said to us "Be not as the hypocrites", which just means "Don't wear a false face – not all the time."

REMEMBRANCE DAY

Remembrance

Who is wearing a poppy? Show me. Who made the poppies? Men and women who have been wounded or blinded in war.

There is nothing thrilling or glorious about war. It is mostly very dull – sometimes very miserable and horrible. The war which was fought when I was a little boy was mostly fought in France or Belgium – much of it in an area called Flanders. During the cold, dark winters, the soldiers lived in holes dug out of the earth and much of the time were standing around in wet trenches. As they looked out from the trenches, almost all they could see was mud – dark, grey mud. Sometimes they wondered if winter would ever end, they even wondered if God had forgotten all about them. Then one day in spring when they looked out, what do you think they saw? Growing here and there in the mud were a great number of scarlet poppies. When they saw the poppies, they knew that God had not forgotten them, that sooner or later peace would come and they would be able to go back to their homes and their wives and children.

So the poppy was a kind of message of hope to the soldiers to tell them that God still loved them and would love them for ever.

So now we wear poppies on Remembrance Day to remember the sacrifice of those who died and to remind us of God's love for all people – for you and for me.

————— · —————

The computer

I expect you know all about computers, boys and girls – marvellous machines which can add, subtract, multiply; which always remember everything you tell them, and can work out the answers to all sorts of complicated questions.

In a way, each one of you has his or her own little computer inside your head. In it everything you learn is stored up – millions and millions of facts – the rules of football, the words of the Lord's Prayer, how to spell. All you've ever learned is there. Whenever you want, you can pull the fact you need out of your memory. What a wonderful thing memory is. Without it, we'd have to learn everything all over again, every day.

Not only can we remember the things we've experienced ourselves, but also what other people have told us and what we've read in books. Although it was long before you were born, you remember when the Battle of Bannockburn was – 1314. In the same way, though none of you was alive during the Second World War and although I was just a baby during the First, we can all of us remember that these wars happened and what sorrow and suffering they caused, and how much bravery they called forth, and why they were fought. That is important, for we don't remember things just for the sake of remembering. We remember them so as to learn. We remember that the wars were fought so that the world might be free of war and cruelty and want and injustice. The better we remember, the more we will try to make sure that the sacrifices which were made were not made in vain.

You and I can't change the past, but we can learn from it, so that we may help to make the future just and peaceable, as God surely wants it to be. "Hear . . . learn . . . and fear the Lord." *(Deuteronomy 31.12)*

ST ANDREW'S DAY

The Saltire

What is this, boys and girls? I know it's a flag, but what flag? It is the Saint Andrew's Cross, the flag of Scotland, and this is November 30th, St Andrew's Day. I wonder why St. Andrew's flag is blue with a white cross?

Some people say that it is because of something that happened long ago in Scotland. The English King, Athelstane, came up to make war, and he would have won the war too, but when the day of battle came, at a place which is now called Athelstaneford, there appeared in the blue sky a great white cross. This upset the English so much that they turned and ran away back to England. And so the Scots took as their flag one of sky-blue with a white cross on it.

I do not know if that is a true story or not, but I'm glad St. Andrew is our special disciple in Scotland, for he was one of the nicest of Jesus' twelve special friends. He was a humble man who did not push himself forward. He did not like to be in the limelight or the centre of the stage. He was content to take a back seat, just so long as he could be of use to Jesus, and he was. It was he who brought his big brother Simon Peter to Jesus, and he brought other people too.

You and I may not be the cleverest people in the world, nor the best looking, nor the richest. But every member of a team counts, not just the one who scores most goals. Every member of a choir counts, not just the one who sings the solos. Every member of the Church counts, not just the leaders. Every disciple counted, not just the chief one.

Jesus needed Andrew just as much as he needed Peter, James and John; and Jesus needs you and me, and he wants us, every one of us, to help him to do his work in the world.

Three people

I want to tell you about three people.

First, a man who lived almost two thousand years ago. He was a fisherman, a humble, good man. Jesus asked him to follow him and he did, and right away went and brought his brother Simon, and after that brought many others to Jesus. Finally he died, for Jesus' sake, on a cross lying on its side like a great X. He is the patron saint of Russia, of Greece and of Scotland, and his special day is November 30th. Who was he? St. Andrew.

The next person I want to tell you about lived in Scotland four hundred years ago. He died on November 24th, 1572. He was a teacher in a rich man's house, but Jesus called him to be a preacher, and he too brought many, many people in Scotland and in other countries to Jesus. He was so keen that everybody should be able to read the Bible that he made certain that there would be a school and a schoolmaster in every parish. He was a very great Scotsman and was hated by all who hated the truth. When he died, someone said, "Here lies one who never feared the face of man." His name was John Knox.

The third person I want to tell you about is still alive and lives right here. I'm not quite sure about this person – not even sure if it's a boy or a girl, a man or a woman. I'm not sure how old he or she is. There's just one thing I know about this person and it is that Jesus is calling him or her, just as surely as he called Andrew and John Knox. Jesus is asking this person to follow him, to bring others to follow too. Do you want to know who this person is? I'll spell it out. It is Y-O-U. Jesus is asking *you* to follow him, just as he asked St. Andrew and John Knox, and he is asking you to bring others with you – as he is asking me. I'd like to think that some of you boys and girls would become ministers or missionaries, but no matter what you are or do, you can follow Jesus and bring others with you, and you can start today, like St. Andrew, who first found his brother Simon and brought him to Jesus.

ELECTION DAY

Choosing

What happens on Thursday, girls and boys? It's the General Election, when the members of Parliament who will govern our country for the next few years will be elected. To "elect" someone is just to choose them. To use a big word, the person we elect will be our representative. That means that he or she will do for us all the things we can't do for ourselves.

Elections are very exciting. It's rather like musical chairs. There's only one seat in the House of Commons for each part of the country, but there are four or five people, called candidates, all hoping to sit on it. Only one of them will get a seat – the others will be left standing outside. I'm always sorry for the ones who are not chosen; it must be very disappointing after they've tried so hard. I heard of one old lady who voted for all the candidates, so that nobody would be left out. But that won't do. You have to choose just one person.

I wonder if any of you will ever stand for Parliament when you grow up. If you do, I hope you'll be elected. Whether or not you hope to be chosen as an M.P., you'll hope to be chosen for other things – for a place in a team perhaps, or for promotion in the Guides or Scouts or in the Brigades, and later on for a job or a place at University.

Jesus once said a strange thing. He said, "You have not chosen me, but I have chosen you." He was not speaking to one person, or to a few, but to all of us. He wants each of us to be one of his representatives in the world, to do the work he can't do without us. He wants us to be his hands, his feet, his mouth, to be his body, to help and to heal, to give and to serve other people in his name.

———————— · ————————

CLOCK CHANGE DAY

No replays for us Adapted h
Jr-J.

Well, boys and girls, did any of you forget to turn the clock back last night? If so, you must have arrived an hour early for church or Sunday School. I'm always so afraid of forgetting that I turn the clocks and watches in the Manse back an hour on Saturday morning. The time we are supposed to do it is at 2 o'clock in the morning, so that we have the hour between 1 a.m. and 2 a.m. twice over. I doubt if many people get up in the middle of the night just to change the clock.

Actually, it would be rather nice to be able to choose which hour to have twice over. We had rather a good dinner at the Manse yesterday. It would have been splendid once it was over just to put the clock back an hour and start all over again. Some of you would choose to have an hour of your favourite television programme twice over, or the last hour before going to bed, or the hour before getting up.

But, you know, whatever we do with the clock, we can't ever have an hour over again once we've lived it.

In the Horse of the Year show on television, they sometimes replay one of the rounds in slow motion, but no matter how often they replay it, the same mistakes are made every time, the same brick knocked off the wall, the same bar off the top of the gate.

That is true of our lives – the mistakes we make, the evil we do can never be wiped out. We can't have our lives, not even one hour of them, to live over again. You cannot undo the things you did yesterday, nor unsay the things you said. That is why we should always ask God's help, that we may keep our hands from evil and our lips from lies, for, as the Psalmist said, "Yesterday is past." *(Psalm 90.4)*

The twenty-three hour day

Girls and boys, how many hours are there in the day? Twenty-four. How many hours are there in *this* day? Wrong. Only twenty-three. In the middle of the night, all the clocks leapt forward one hour. Next autumn there will be a day with twenty-five hours to make up for it.

Wouldn't it be wonderful if we could choose for ourselves some days to be long and some to be short – school days nice and short; holidays nice and long; wet days short; sunny days long.

But you know, if we ask Jesus to help us to face each day with courage and kindness and cheerfulness, he will, and, sure of his companionship, every day will be worth living, even the dreariest, wettest Monday when we have an exam, and a cold coming.

Jesus once said, and he meant it, "I am with you *always*."

And that means every day from Sunday to Saturday every week, always and for ever.

———————— · ————————

THE SCHOOL YEAR

BEGINNING OF TERM

Back to school

Soon you'll be going back to school, girls and boys. It is not much fun to think that the holidays are over for another year. You may look enviously at those who left school at the end of the Summer Term. They have either started working, doing something new and interesting, or they are having extra holidays before going to College or University. They're lucky, aren't they? Still, if you work hard, your turn will come too, and you will soon have left your school-days behind you.

But, do you know, there are some folks who go to school all their lives, even when they're quite old – thirty, forty, fifty, even sixty years old? You might think that they must be very stupid to have to go to school all their lives. They're not. They're very, very clever. Have you guessed who they are? They are your teachers; back for the nth time to school with you, and no hope of leaving until they're ready to retire. If you're not looking forward to the new term, think what it must be like for them.

Of course, none of us stop learning. Although we leave school, it is just to become students or apprentices, or to learn some job elsewhere. Even after we have become masters of our job, or qualified in our professions, we'll have to go on learning right to the end. That's the way life is. Fortunately, there are lots of helpful people willing to give us the benefit of their experience.

Life itself is in some ways just like a big school. There are some pretty hard tests in it for us and some difficult lessons for us to learn. But God hasn't left us to face it alone The Lord Jesus Christ came and lived our life, faced our temptations and sorrows, and died our death, and he is willing to help us. That is what he meant when once he said, "Learn of me." If we do, I don't think we'll fail in the School of Life.

Compensations

There is a sad day coming quite soon for you, girls and boys, the first day of school after the holidays. As you make your way to school feeling a little miserable, it may cheer you up to remember that it is an even harder day for your teachers. They have got to go back to school too, and, whereas you can look forward to the day when you leave school, they have got to go to school all their lives!

The other thing to think about is that even if it is a sad day for you and a sadder for the teacher, it is a very glad day for some other people – for the lady in the flat downstairs who was becoming a little tired of the noise you made when you were on holiday; for the park ranger, who was having trouble making sure you didn't play football in the wrong places; even for your mothers, who were growing a little weary of thinking up things for you to do and having you around the house all day.

There are compensations for you, too, in going back to school. You will have old friends to meet, new books to read and some subjects that are fun, and afternoons on the sports field. Another happy thought is that there is always the end of term to look forward to. The very first day after the summer holidays is the beginning of the Christmas term, the first day after the Christmas holidays is the Easter term, and the first day after the Easter holidays is the Summer term. That is how it goes. After Summer holidays there comes Christmas; after Christmas, Easter; after Easter Summer again. The end of every good thing is the beginning of something even better. After school, University, which is great fun; after University, work, which can be fun too; then marriage and children and grandchildren, and after life itself, the life everlasting. It is something like this that is meant by the words of our text, "Behold, I make all things new." *(Revelation 21.5)*

The first day at school

Last week a little boy went to school for the first time. After a few minutes, he decided he'd like to see his mother, so he said, 'I'm going home." The teacher explained that he couldn't go home until the end of the day. He thought for a while and decided to meet the teacher half way, so he said, "Well, I'll stick it till play-time." Actually, he's sticking it still and he will stick it for twelve long years and for longer than that if he goes to University. He will learn all sorts of things before he is done, but he learned one of the most important things on that first day. He learned that in school, and in life, there are some things you've got to stick, whether you like them or not.

There are lots of things in life which are great fun. But there are other things you've just got to put up with – homework, dish-washing, piano practice, illness.

There's a word the Bible uses: to "endure." That just means to stick at something or to bear something that's hard. That is the word St. Paul used when he wrote in a letter to his friend, Timothy, "Endure hardship as a good soldier of Jesus Christ."

Jesus himself endured all sorts of hard things for our sakes and at last endured death itself.

END OF TERM

The cattle show

This is a great time of year for prize-givings – at school, at Sunday School or at Sports Day.

Recently I saw some prize-winners, but they were very odd prize-winners. They didn't know that they were entered for a prize and they didn't know that they had won one. Indeed, they will never know, which seems rather a shame.

Where was I? At a cattle show. Who were the prize-winners? Cows and sheep, horses and donkeys, pigs and goats. There they were, fine animals with first prize rosettes. Some of them had won lovely silver cups, but they didn't know it and they didn't care. They would just as soon have been at home on the farm eating grass.

I'm rather glad I'm not an animal. I wouldn't want to be be a pig or a goat or a donkey – not even a prize pig or a prize goat or a prize donkey. But in one way we would be wise if we were like the animals – if we didn't worry about the prizes, but were just as good as we could be, and did as well as we could do. If we did, then it wouldn't matter if we got any prizes or not.

At the show they had clever farmers from all over the country to judge the cattle and the sheep. God is *our* judge, and if we do our very best to obey him and to follow the example of Jesus, God will say to us at the last, "Well done," and that will be the best prize of all.

—————— · ——————

The school report

Are you afraid of a piece of paper? There's one piece of paper which most of you have received recently, and you didn't look forward to receiving it. I've got one in my hand. It's not a threatening letter or a Black Spot such as Long John Silver got from Blind Pugh. It's a report card. It's meant to tell your father and mother how you are getting on at school Somehow parents always expect you to do better than you do.

I sometimes think that it is a little one-sided. It is all very well for the teachers to give their opinions of the pupils. How would the grown-ups like it if the pupils gave a report on their teachers at the end of every year? Or if the children gave a report card on their parents? How many marks would you give your father for good temper or for keeping the grass cut? What percentage would you give your mother for baking or sewing on buttons? Do you remember the morning she burned the toast? If it's wet this afternoon you can all have some fun writing out report cards for each other. It might help us all to do better just so long as we don't quarrel about it. It is good for us at times to ask ourselves what other people think about us.

Most importantly we should ask ourselves what God thinks of us and and we should make up our minds to live so that we can be sure that he will be pleased with what he sees.

SCHOOL HOLIDAYS

The passport

Well, boys and girls, are you glad your holidays have begun? I'll tell you who are even more glad – your teachers!

Most of you know where you are going for your holidays. It is good to have a change from home sometimes. It's most exciting of all if you are going abroad to France perhaps, or Belgium, or Spain, or Switzerland. If you are going abroad, I hope you are all prepared, that you have bought your tickets and got your supplies of the exciting-looking foreign money. Then there is something else you must have if you're going to a foreign country. I wonder if you know what it is? Right! It's a passport. Here is mine.

It is a very grand little book, with eight lions on the outside, and inside there is a message from the Queen saying that I must be given every help and protection wherever I may go – which is very nice of Her Majesty. If you are going abroad this summer, I hope you have your passport all ready, otherwise you may not be allowed into the foreign country you have chosen.

I would gladly lend you mine, but it wouldn't be of any use. I wonder if you know why? First of all there is the number. Mine is 309445 and nobody else in the world has that number but me. Inside my passport there are two other things which are mine alone – one is my signature which nobody could copy exactly, even if they wished to. The other thing is my face – nobody else in the world has a face just like mine, which is perhaps a good thing!

When God made us, he made us all different. Each of us is a one-off. It is possible to make stamps by the million, all alike, and coins, pens and pencils, books and newspapers so that you could not tell one from the other. But when God made us, he made us one by one and every one different.

We don't need a passport to go into his Kingdom, nor a photograph to prove who we are – he doesn't even give us a number. He knows each of us by our own name. He once said, "I have called you by name. You are mine." *(Isaiah 43.1)*

———————— · ————————

The perfume factory

Last summer we visited a factory in France. That seems a funny thing to do on a holiday to visit a factory, but this was not a noisy, smelly factory. It was very quiet, set right in the heart of the country, and everywhere there were the most delicious smells. It was a perfume factory. We were told all sorts of interesting things about it. For example, it takes three tons of rose petals to make one litre of perfume essence. There must be millions of petals in three tons and each has to give up its little bit of sweetness for the sake of the whole.

One of the things which struck us at the perfume factory was how tidy and neat everything was. With tons of rose petals you might think it wouldn't matter if one petal was wasted. But the perfume manufacturers know that if they are not careful to get the tiny drop of perfume from every single petal, they would soon have no perfume at all.

Today you are going to be given your prizes for attending church regularly. Sometimes it may seem to you that it can't matter very much whether you are at church or not, to sing the hymns and join in the prayers and worship. There are so many others in church that it can't possibly matter whether you are here or not. But it does matter. It is all of our praises and prayers and worship *together* that make up the praises and prayers of the church. Every single person is needed – God needs you, every one.

The villagers of Eyam

There is a little village in Derbyshire called Eyam. It is a famous little village because of something which happened there just over three hundred years ago. It was something very sad, which the villagers faced with great bravery.

One day in 1666 there arrived in Eyam some cloth from London. The tailor who received the cloth did not know it, but in the cloth were the germs of a terrible illness which was raging in London at the time – an illness called the Plague. Very soon the tailor took ill and died. The minister of the church in Eyam at once guessed what had happened. He gathered everyone in the village together and told them that the Plague had come to their village. He told them that if they wanted to be selfish, they could all run away from the village. But if they did, they might spread the Plague all over the north of England. So the minister asked them, for the sake of others, to cut themselves off from all contact with the outside world. This they did for over a year. No one left the village or came into it. Food and medicines were brought and left where the villagers could find them. Almost everyone in Eyam became ill, but nobody left the village and no one came in. Not a single person in the rest of Derbyshire caught the disease.

Once a year the people of Eyam hold a service in the parish church to give thanks for the self-denial and courage of their ancestors.

It is always good to remember courage and unselfishness. We can give thanks that three hundred years ago the people of Eyam were kind and good and brave enough to make sure that the evil thing which had come among them did not spread to other people.

Sometimes horrid things come into all our lives – lies, cruel stories about other people, unclean things, – things every bit as bad as the germs of the Plague. We can't help that, but when it happens, let us make sure of one thing – that we don't pass on to others that which is untrue, or unkind, or unclean. We can make sure that the Plague doesn't spread.

———————————— · ————————————

The day of small things

One Sunday when we were on holiday, we worshipped in the little church in the village where we were staying, and we heard a very sad story.

It seems that this little church needed a new organ, so the people in the village all gave as much money as they could afford, and a new organ was bought, a nice, new, electric organ. There was a lot of excitement when Sunday came and the new organ was to be played for the first time. All the people were in church and the minister was ready. The organist went in and sat down at the organ, switched it on, pressed his hands on the keys – and nothing happened. He twiddled the knobs, he switched on; off; and nothing happened, not a note, not a squeak, not a whisper – just silence. Everything was tried, but it was no use. They had to wait until Monday and fetch someone down from Glasgow. He came and took the organ apart, and do you know all that was wrong? There was a little hole in the organ about the size of a ten pence piece, and through the hole had wandered an inquisitive little mouse. It had liked the look of one of the wires, so it had chewed through it and broken the supply of electricity to the organ.

One little hole, one little mouse, one little meal, and the organ was silenced.

Little things matter. A little lie, a little cruelty, a little discourtesy can cause all sorts of trouble.

Small things matter – for good and for bad.

———————————— · ————————————

Read the maker's instructions

Girls and boys, what's the first thing you should do when you get something new, like a toy, or a kit for making aeroplanes or ships? What should you read before beginning to use them? You've guessed it – the maker's instructions.

A friend of mine was going on holiday to a very lovely part of Italy – the Dolomites. He thought it would be nice to have lots of pictures of his holiday to look at in the long, dark winter nights. So he bought a new camera – a little flat rectangular one. He was too busy enjoying his holiday to bother to read the booklet of instructions which came with the camera, but he took lots of pictures of mountains and waterfalls, of quaint-looking houses and ancient castles. Once he got home, he could hardly wait to get his pictures developed and printed. He took the film to a chemist and was quite excited when he collected the pictures – all forty of them. But when he opened the packet, there were no pictures of mountains or waterfalls, of curious-looking houses or castles. All he had were forty pictures which looked exactly alike. Each was of two dark circles, one inside the other, surrounded by a white bit, which looked exactly like an eye, and that is exactly what it was. Instead of pointing the camera outwards at the pictures he wanted to take, he had faced it inwards on his own eye. He wishes now that he had read the maker's instructions.

Who was your maker, boys and girls? You know the answer to that question, don't you? It was God, of course; and God who made us has not left us without directions on how life should be lived. He has given us "maker's instructions" – the Bible. The ten commandments and the teaching of Jesus are our maker's instructions. If we follow them, we shall live our lives to the full and be as much use as we can be to God and other people.

Read your maker's instructions and obey them. They're all here in the Bible. That's what St. Paul meant when he wrote to Timothy, "All Scripture is inspired by God and is useful for teaching the truth and giving instructions for right living." *(2 Timothy 3.16)*

--- · ---

Relations

How many uncles do you have? Some children have lots of uncles, while others have only one. Some have none at all, which is a pity as uncles are mostly nice, kind people and are very handy at holiday times.

Almost two thousand years ago some boys and girls in Palestine had the most wonderful uncle anybody ever had, for their uncle was Jesus. We know that Jesus had brothers and sisters and we can be sure that their children loved their Uncle Jesus very much indeed.

Well, we can't have Jesus for our uncle, but we can have him as our friend and saviour, and as a brother, for he taught us to call his Father, our Father. When Jesus went back to Heaven he said to his friends, "I'm going back to my Father and to your Father, to my God and to your God." Those who have the same Father are brothers and sisters, members of the same great family of God. If we remembered that always, that we are brothers and sisters of the Lord Jesus Christ, it would help us to be truthful and kind and generous and pure – like him.

--- · ---

Holiday weather

We have been on holiday for the last two weeks, boys and girls. We weren't in the south of France. We weren't in Spain or Italy. We were near Campbeltown in Argyllshire, but the sun shone every day from morning to night. Mark you, you couldn't see it on account of the rain and the fog, but it was there, just the same as in France or Spain or Italy. Above the clouds and the mist, the sky is as blue and the sun shines as brightly in Scotland as anywhere else in the world. If you go up in an aeroplane on even the foggiest or rainiest day, as soon as you rise above the clouds the sky is blue and the sun is bright.

People sometimes say that there is no God, just because they can't see him. But he is there, just the same, as surely as the sun is shining above the clouds.

Just as the sun, even in Scotland, sometimes breaks through the clouds, so God once appeared to men in Jesus Christ. So now we know what God is like, and we know that when we see him one day, we'll find that he is exactly like Jesus.

EVERYDAY THINGS

TRANSPORT

A road sign

Boys and girls, when I'm driving I try to obey the Highway Code and the road signs I see along the way. When a notice says, "SLOW", I go slowly; when one says, "GIVE WAY", I give way; when it says, "LOOK RIGHT", I look right, and when it says, "LOOK LEFT", I look left. But the other day I saw a notice which nobody could obey. Do you know what it said? "LOOK BOTH WAYS". Well, you can look right and then left but you can try for a thousand years and you can't look both ways at once, unless you are like the Pushmi–Pullyu in *Dr. Dolittle* and have two heads; or unless you are like your teachers, for all teachers seem to have eyes in the back of their heads! But ordinary folk like us, who have just two eyes in the front of our heads, can look left or right, but never both ways. You've got to choose.

And that is true of all your life. You've got to choose – to choose between truth and lies, between goodness and badness, between cruelty and kindness, between God and self.

Jesus once said "Nobody can serve two masters; you cannot serve God and selfishness." Make up your mind then, and make up your mind to trust and to love and to obey the only master who is worth trusting and loving and obeying -the Lord Jesus Christ.

———————— · ————————

Another road sign

Another road sign for you, boys and girls! At the side of some country roads there are little mounds of gravel, or sometimes

metal bins, and they are labelled "GRIT FOR THE ROAD".
Wherever you see this notice, there will be a pile of sand with
some salt in it. It is meant for use when there is a sudden freeze-up
and the road becomes slippery. It would be no use to have to go
off to hunt for grit to make the road useable after it had frozen
over. It has to be all ready to hand.

So it is when we come to a slippery place in life, when we have
to face pain, or difficulty or temptation. It is no use then
wondering where we can get help. We've got to know where to
turn and to whom. When our need is greatest we can always turn
to God and to his help and strength and love, made free to us in
Jesus Christ his son. There's grit for the road of life – free and
plenty for all. That is what God meant when he said to Paul, "My
grace is all you need, for my power is strongest when you are
weak." *(2 Corinthians 12.9)*

Easter road signs

I want to try an experiment. I'm going to say a word and ask you
to say out loud what that word suggests to you. For example, if I
say "night", you might say "day"; "ham" – "eggs". If I say
"school", you *might* say "happiness".

Ready? As soon as I say this word, shout out your reply.
"Easter" – ?

Wrong! Easter is not about eggs, or rabbits, or chickens, or
holidays. It's about death. You're not supposed to think much
about death, but you do, you can't help it. What Easter says about
death is that it is not the end. It is the door through which Christ
passed, and in his company we too can pass through it.

Some of you are very keen on cars. Before long you will be
applying for your driving licence. When you do you will have to
pass a test on the Highway Code, and one of the things you will be
asked is the meaning of the various road signs.

This sign means "NO THROUGH ROAD".

Here's another one which is not quite so common. That means "CLEARWAY", that nothing is allowed to block the road. Before Christ came, when people thought about death, they thought that there was no road through it, that it was a "dead end". But not any more, not since Jesus died and rose again. Now we know that there is a "clear way" through death and on for ever. For Jesus has gone before us as he promised.

Death is not a "NO THROUGH ROAD" – a dead end, but a "CLEAR WAY" through to life with Christ for ever.

Jesus said, "After I am risen I will go before you." *(Mark 14.28)*

One-way streets

You know what a one-way street is, don't you? It's a street where traffic is allowed to go only in one direction, and no one can drive the other way along it. At least they *can* drive the other way, and sometimes they do, in spite of all the signs. The other day I saw a van doing it. Motorists hooted at it and policemen waved at it to stop, for it is against the law to do that, and it can only end in trouble all round.

That is how it is with God's law. You *can* break it if you want. You needn't bother with the Church, you can tell lies and be cruel. At first it seems that nothing is going to happen to you, that you are going to get away with it. But sooner or later, if you break God's law, you'll cause the most dreadful trouble to yourself and to everybody else.

It's sometimes hard to know what to do in life. The signs are all a bit confusing. That is why Jesus came and said "Follow me." If we do, we shall not go wrong. The old prophet Hosea knew that, for once he said, "The Lord's ways are right." *(Hosea 14.9)*

Kerb drill

Do you know your kerb drill, boys and girls? I hope you do. It's very important. "Look right, look left, look right again and if the road is clear walk straight across." If you always follow the kerb drill you should be all right.

But the other day a boy had to be taken to hospital. He wasn't seriously ill, but he had a cut on his head. The nurse in charge of the ward said to him, "How did this happen? Did you forget your kerb drill?" "No," he said, "I looked right, looked left and looked right again. Then I stepped off the pavement and a slate fell off a roof and hit me." So the nurse said, "Next time you'll need to look up, as well as right and left."

Well, luckily slates don't often fall off roofs. But people, boys and girls and grown-ups too, would be better to look up sometimes. If we did we might say what the Psalmist said, "When I look at the sky which you have made, at the moon and the stars which you set in their places, what is man that you think of him?"

Look up at the stars some of these fine nights, and at the moon, or watch a sunset sometimes. When you do, think of the God who made all that beauty, and made us to enjoy it. That same God who has come very near to us in Jesus Christ.

L for Learner

I have an old, somewhat battered car, boys and girls. It is ten years old, and has travelled nearly eighty thousand miles. I usually do most of the driving, but recently I have been trying to teach two of my sons to drive. Before I could take them out on their Provisional Driving Licences, I had to put one "L plate" – L standing for Learner – on the front, and one on the back of the car.

The "L plates" looked rather funny when they were on it. One could almost hear the car say, "What? Me a Learner? What a nerve! Call these newfangled little cars learners if you like, but not me." I think it must have felt just as you big boys and girls might feel if you were called infants. When you think of it, it's a little mean to label the car as a learner when it's only its driver who is.

But my poor old car need not have been so cross. There is no shame in being a learner. Indeed, the shame is if we stop learning. Even after you leave school and college you must go on learning about this wonderful world, about your job, about books, and about people. In fact, we ought to go on learning about life all our lives, wearing invisible "L plates" from babyhood to old age. Above all, we should go on learning about Jesus and his loving purposes for us. He himself once said, "Learn of me." *(Matthew 11.29)*

————— · —————

Learning to drive

A little boy once saw a car with an "L plate" on it. Do you know what that means? He didn't, so very sensibly he asked his mother. She explained that it meant that the driver was a learner. A few days later the boy saw a car with the letters "GB" on it.

So he said to his mother, "I know what that means," and when she asked "What?", he said, "It means 'Getting better'."

Well, you and I are not learning how to drive. I learned long ago and it will be a while before you are allowed to learn. But we are all of us learning all our lives, from the time we are little babies, till the time we are quite old. We have to learn to walk and to speak, to wash and to dress. Later on at school we learn how to read and write and count and all sorts of clever things. We learn to ride a bicycle, to speak French, to play the piano perhaps, or to sing. After you leave school you will go on learning about your trade or profession, learning about this wonderful world and the people in it, learning about life and its meaning. We all ought to wear "L plates" from babyhood until we die. We're all learners in one way or another every day.

There is one sure way of learning the important things and learning them in the right way, and that is to learn from Jesus. That is how we can make sure not only that we ourselves get better every day, but that our nation and our world get better too.

Learn from Jesus. (Show "L plate".)

Get Better. (Show 'GB" sign.)

Every time you see a car with an "L plate " on it, decide again to learn from Jesus. Every time you see one with a "GB" sticker, ask Jesus to help you to get better.

Seat-belts

Boys and girls, when you are young you usually have to wear the clothes your mother buys for you. One of the good things about being grown up is that you can more or less wear what you like.

But there's one place where I have to wear something whether I like it or not (and some people don't like it.) But if I don't wear it, one day soon a policeman will stop my car and I'll have to go to court and pay a fine, or go to prison, or at least get a good row. What is it I have to wear whenever I am in a car? A seat-belt.

I'm sure the government is quite right to make the wearing of seat-belts compulsory. It may be a bit of a nuisance, but it is for our own good, so that if we are in an accident we won't be badly hurt.

The laws of the land are meant to help us and not to hurt us.

So are the laws of God.

It may seem to us at times that it would make life easier if we told a lie, or that it would be fun to steal something. It would not really. God has told us in the ten commandments not to lie or to steal. And what God tell us to do or not to do is always for our own good. God has even given us a little policeman to tell us when we're doing wrong things and to warn us not to. The policeman is called Conscience. It is very silly to disobey policeman Conscience. It always leads to trouble.

If we are wise we'll learn God's commandments and obey them, learn about Jesus and follow his example. If we do we shall do nothing to hurt ourselves nor anybody else.

Elephants

Every car, every van and lorry, every motor-cycle in this country has to have a number plate, but in one country in Africa elephants also have number plates.

Some years ago, the government of Uganda wanted to know how many elephants there were and how far they wandered, and they decided the only thing to do was to put a number on each one. But how do you do it? A car or a cycle will stand still while you put on a number plate, but not an elephant.

Well, what they did was this. They shot the elephant with a little arrow with a drug on the tip. The elephant hardly even felt the prick, but the drug made him feel sleepy. Soon he lay down and fell fast asleep. The men crept up and painted a number on his side, about a yard long. When the elephant woke up it didn't know that anything had happened, but ever after it carried its number plate on its side.

The scheme worked. One elephant was seen a thousand miles away from the place where he got his number plate. Another visited a neighbouring country three times.

Well, girls and boys, we don't carry number plates, but God who has made us knows each one of us, knows us as we are, and where we are, and how we are. He will never forget us, nor leave us, nor let us go. He said once, "I have called you by name, you are mine." *(Isaiah 43.1)*

The bridge to God

What's the longest bridge you've ever been over, boys and girls? One over a river perhaps, like the Forth; or over a deep valley, like some of the railway viaducts; or even over a lake, as in some of the Hydro-Electric schemes? There is actually a bridge which goes over the Atlantic Ocean. It is from the island of Seil to the mainland. It's not a very long bridge, for it's built over only a tiny bit of the Atlantic Ocean.

But quite soon now another bridge is to be taken over the Atlantic all the way to America. To be honest, it is not going to be built across the Atlantic. It is going to sail across in a ship. It is London Bridge, and it hasn't fallen down. It has been sold for a million pounds and is being taken down bit by bit to be sailed across to America. But it will be a long time before men will be able to build a bridge right across the Atlantic. It is two thousand miles across, and the longest bridge in the world so far is in China, and it is only eighty-nine miles long!

Bridges are wonderful things. They carry us over great, deep rivers and valleys we couldn't possibly cross without them. That is why the most wonderful bridge in the world is the one built long ago by God. There was a great gulf between us and God, a gulf had made by our own rebellion against him. We couldn't get over that gulf, so God built a bridge to let us reach him. That is what St. Paul meant when he said, "There is one God, and one mediator between God and men, the man Christ Jesus." For the word "mediator" just means bridge, and the one bridge between God and men is Jesus Christ. The only way you and I can reach God is through Jesus Christ our Lord. "For there is one God, and one mediator between God and men, the man Christ Jesus." *(1 Timothy 2.5)*

The Transport Museum

Have you ever been to the Transport Museum in Glasgow? It is well worth a visit. They have every sort of transport from roller skates to railway engines, trams and buses, models of ships, traction engines, steam locomotives, a gypsy caravan, motor cars more than eighty years old, and a mail coach. It's all very interesting but there is just one snag. Every one of the vehicles is in splendid working order, but not one of them is going anywhere. Transport is not for looking at – it is for using.

That applies to other things too. The Cathedral is a lovely building to look at. Thirty thousand tourists come to see it every year, but it is not just meant to be looked at. It is meant to be used for worship.

Here is a fine Bible. It has nice covers and is beautifully bound, but every page might as well be blank unless somebody reads it.

The Bible and the Church, like different forms of transport, are not just for looking at. They are for using to help us on our way through life.

Sundays only

Are you good at looking up railway timetables? I'm not. The other Monday I was going quite a distance by train and I looked up the timetable and found a fast train which left just after breakfast. I thought that would be fine, but when I looked closer there was a small ^x at it and after searching for a while I discovered that the small ^x meant "Saturdays only". That wasn't any use, so I looked again and found one almost as suitable but a little earlier. It didn't have an ^x. It had a + and after a hunt I found that that meant "Except Mondays". That wasn't any use either. Then there were some trains marked **X**, which meant Wednesdays and Saturdays only. Finally it seemed that there was hardly one train left which went every day. I dare say British Railways do their best, but it is all very confusing. It would be so much easier if *every* train ran *every* day. We wouldn't make nearly so many mistakes.

It is a pity trains aren't the same every day. It is a greater pity when people aren't. There are people, quite a lot of them, and boys and girls too, who are as different from one day to another as chalk is from cheese. One day they're kind. The next day they're cruel. One day they're happy. The next day they're miserable. One day they're good-tempered. The next day they're cross. You just never know how you're going to find them. Just like the trains, they're never the same two days running. There are even people, and boys and girls, who try to be good and follow Christ only on one day of the week. They might be called "Sundays only" Christians. They are not much use to Christ. He wants us to love and serve and follow him not one day in the week, but every day. Do you remember what he said? "Daily . . . follow me." *(Luke 9.23)*

Trains

How many of you have been on a train? You have probably been on a train drawn by a diesel or an electric engine, but they're not real trains! The real trains were drawn by steam – I remember steam engines for the great clouds of steam, and screaming whistles, and the glare from the fire reflected in the driver's and fireman's faces. For one hundred and fifty years all the trains in Britain were driven by steam.

The inventor of the steam engine was a Scot from Greenock called James Watt. It is said that he got his idea when he watched the steam of boiling water lift the lid of his mother's kettle. From that one incident came all the railway lines. All the millions of people who travelled by steam train and sent their goods by train were in debt to this one man.

But fashion changes and new inventions replace the old. James Watt's steam engine is now quite out of date.

But there was one person whose ideas never go out of date; one life lived on earth which will never lose its power, the life of Jesus of Nazareth. He is as alive, as modern, as able and ready to help as he was when he lived on earth almost two thousand years ago. "He is able to save, now and always." *(Hebrews 7.25)*

Snow

Last week roads were blocked, trains were buried, buses were lost, cars disappeared. What caused the trouble? There wasn't an earthquake or a volcanic eruption. All the trouble was caused by one thing with a short name of only four letters. It was snow, of course. There's still a lot of it about, but if I asked you to go out and bring me back one snowflake, you couldn't do it. As soon as you took it onto your hand it would melt. Each snowflake is very, very small, so light that you couldn't possibly weigh it. Yet all of those great heaps of snow in the High Street, the ten- and twenty-foot drifts in the country, are all made up of these tiny little snowflakes, millions and millions of them. One snowflake never did anyone any harm, but once another falls and then another, they will build up to those huge piles which have caused such trouble.

So it is with many little things. A little lie seems hardly worth bothering about, but add one lie to another, and soon an awful lot of harm will be done. One cigarette can't kill you, but if you have another and another you can shorten your life.

So it is with little good things. If one of us did one kind thing today for Jesus' sake it might not seem very important, but if all of us did, we would make our town a better place to live.

When you think of the great big world, with all of the sad and cruel things that happen in it, you might ask yourself "What can one person do to help?" But once we all get together, as we do in church, it is wonderful how much we can accomplish, for Christ's sake, to help other people.

"A1" at Lloyds

We have all been sorry about the recent heavy loss of life at sea, particularly about the sinking of the fishing trawlers. Once upon a time even more ships were lost, partly because many ships were going to sea with rotten old hulls, twisted rudders and masts, and rigging in poor condition. Finally, some businessmen in London who were interested in ships and shipping got together to form a company called Lloyds. They persuaded the government to pass a law that no British ship might go to sea unless it had been passed as in good condition.

Now every ship is examined to see if its hull is sound. If it is, it is given the letter "A". If it is not quite sound, it is classed as "B", and as "C" if it is even worse. Then all of the ship's other equipment is examined. It is given a number "1" if it is perfect, "2" if it has some defect, and "3" if it is worse than that. So if a ship is classified as "A1 at Lloyds", it means that it is perfect, both in its hull and its equipment. There is no use having a ship with a good hull if its rigging is rotten and its steering gear won't work. The only kind of ship worth sailing in is one that is "A1 at Lloyds".

So it is too with our lives. It is of no use having great strong bodies and clever brains if our hearts and souls are all twisted and decayed. The only life worth living is the life modelled on the life of Jesus Christ who said, "Be ye therefore perfect, even as your Father which is in Heaven is perfect." Do not be satisfied to be a "B2" or a "C3" person. Try hard to be the best that you can be – "A1". That is what God wants you to be, and will help you to be, if you ask him.

A walking stick

What is this I have in my hand? A walking stick? That is what people call it anyway, but I've always thought that it was a very silly name. Did any of you ever see a stick walking? I never did. Try it with a walking stick at home. Stand it up against a wall and say to it, "Go on! Walk!" Do you know what will happen? Nothing at all. Why, even a little baby can do better. If he can't walk, he can crawl, or at the very least he can wriggle. But a walking stick can do nothing. Lay it on the floor and say, "Go on. If you can't walk, crawl, or at least wriggle." You know what will happen. Nothing at all! Walking stick, indeed! It can't walk a step – not, that is, unless it is in someone's hand. By itself, it is of no use in the world.

Christ tells us that we are – just like the walking stick – quite helpless by ourselves. We can eat and drink, and walk and talk of course, but we can do nothing lasting or worthwhile unless we do it with him. It is only as we put ourselves into the hands of Christ that he can use us for his own very great and wonderful purposes. Only as we ask him to use us do we become what we were meant to become – his servants and his friends. For Jesus said, "Abide in me, and I in you . . . , without me ye can do nothing." *(John 15.4)*

POWER

Telephones

When I was young, girls and boys, telephones were all black and shiny and heavy. Nowadays you can have any colour you please, blue, yellow, red, green, grey or black. You can have push-button telephones, loudspeaker telephones, cordless telephones, video-telephones, and even one which can talk to a computer.

Now, we at the Manse don't have a trimphone, nor a push-button phone. All we have, and all we want or need, is a good old-fashioned phone with a nice clear, loud bell. For what matters is not what colour of telephone you have, nor what sort of noise the bell makes. What matters is what happens when you lift the phone and hear what the person who wants to speak to you has to say.

There was another bell we all heard this morning which told us that someone very important wanted to speak to us. Which bell was that? The church bell, of course, and the church bell rings to tell us that God wants to speak to us.

But listening to that bell does us no more good than listening to the phone bell. It is when the church bell stops that God speaks to us in our prayers and in the Bible. Long ago, a young boy, Samuel, thought he heard someone call him and he said, "Speak, Lord, for your servant is listening."

If we say the same, then, although we won't hear God speak out loud with our ears, we'll hear him speak in our hearts and know that he is here.

The magic door

In a shop the other day, I saw a wonderful door. It had no handles and no door knob. If you had stood looking at it, you might have wondered, "How in the world shall I ever get through that?" But I watched some other people. They marched up to the door as bravely as you like, and when they were close to it, it swung open of its own accord. They didn't have to push it or anything. It may be done by an invisible beam, or the mat you stand on, but it's a great help when you're carrying two big parcels.

You might think that is a very modern invention, but, you know, there was one like that in the Bible. You can read about it in the Book of Acts, chapter twelve, verse ten.

It tells there how St. Peter was once in prison, as many other good men have been. The day came when Peter was told by an angel that he could go free. Peter knew that there was a big iron gate to the prison. If he'd sat in his cell and said, "Oh, what's the use? I'll never get through the big iron gate," he would never have got out. But Peter trusted God and when he was told to, he walked right up to the iron gate and, as he did, the iron gate opened of its own accord.

The lesson in all this is that there's no use sitting thinking about your difficulties and problems. Get up and face them bravely and they disappear.

If we obey God and do what is right and true and kind, then, when we come to them – just like the automatic doors at the shop – the iron gates will open of their own accord.

———————— · ————————

Sunlight

Boys and girls, the most powerful thing in the world is coming right through the church windows. Don't be afraid. If it strikes you, it won't hurt. What is it?

It is coming through the South window, and later on it will come through the West window.

It is sunshine. The rays of the sun don't seem very strong, but all sorts of things draw power from them. The American Skylab is drawing all its power, three thousand watts, from the sun. The astronauts have a very powerful oven, it can even melt metals. It is called a Solar Furnace, because it draws its terrific heat, not from gas or electricity, but from the sun.

Mark you, if your mother were to put out the roast of beef, or the potatoes, hoping the sun would cook them, you would not get your dinner for a long, long time – even if the dog didn't run away with it! In order to use the sun's rays, the astronauts had to catch them on a solar panel.

If you and I are to receive the power of God, we must open our hearts and our lives to him. We must be like the first disciples, to whom the Spirit of God came at the first Pentecost, the first birthday of the Church. It came when the disciples joined together to pray.

Organ pipes

It was fun when the BBC were here a few weeks ago to record our service for the radio. But they weren't very nice to me. They said, would I mind not singing. I said, "Why?". Do you know what they said? "Because you can't."

I can't play the piano, nor the oboe, nor the Dolmetch Descant Recorder, nor the bagpipes. But the other day I came into church when our organ was in pieces, being cleaned and repaired. There was nobody looking, so I had a go and found I could play the organ – or at least a bit of it. So I've brought the bit I can play with me today. Would you like to hear me play it?

(Blow into a very small organ pipe.)

I asked the organist how many little pipes like this there are and he said, "Nine hundred and eighty." I asked him if I could keep this one little bit, but, you know, he wouldn't let me. He said he needed it and that if he let me keep it, the organ would not sound right. So he said I could have one last go and then I must hand it back.

A good organist needs every little bit of the organ and he knows if even one is missing.

God is like that. He has so many people, men and women and boys and girls, that you'd think he would never miss one.

But he does. He loves each of us so much that he sent Jesus into the world to live for us and to die for us, so that not one of us might be lost.

That is what Jesus meant when he said, "I am going to prepare a place for you, so that you will be where I am." *(John 14.2)*

————————— · —————————

The electric plug

I've something in my hand, boys and girls. You all have one at home, probably you have lots of them, but it is rather a wonderful thing. You could get heat through it and you could get enough cold to make ice. You could use it to get dirt, horrid, nasty dirt, and you could use it to make things clean, whiter than white. You could use it to get pictures, and music and light, and even a sermon.

Do you know what it is? An electric plug. You could use it for a vacuum-cleaner and get dirt, for a washing-machine and get things clean, for a refrigerator and get cold, and for a fire and get heat. You could use it for a lamp, or a television set, or a radio. It's a wonderful thing.

There is something far more wonderful in your house. It is sometimes good and sometimes naughty, sometimes clean and sometimes dirty, sometimes happy and sometimes miserable. It is the most wonderful thing in the world – a boy or a girl. There is hardly anything a boy or girl can't do or be, if they really try. But, like every other wonderful thing, they can be wonderfully good or wonderfully bad.

What worried St. James was that out of the same mouth could come truth and lies, kind words and cruel. The same lips could pray to God and could say mean and false things about people. "Words of thanksgiving and cursing pour out from the same mouth." *(James 3.10)*

How can we be always the best that we can be? How can we be sure that all our powers and gifts will always be used for good purposes?

There is only one way, and that is to put them, and to put ourselves, into the hands of God. Then our lives will be good and true and useful to God and to all around us.

———————— · ————————

Television

Well, girls and boys, everything is here for tonight's television service – the scaffolding, the lights, the cables with two hundred thousand watts, the Outside Broadcast van, everything except the two most important things – the cameras and the microphones. Do you know why they're not here? They were all being used yesterday for the Scottish Cup Final when Rangers beat Celtic – or was it the other way about? It is funny to think that the self-same cameras which were watching the football crowds at Hampden will be looking at us tonight. I hope they don't send out the pictures from Hampden – or the sound – instead of our "Songs of Praise". It would be awful if the BBC got the pictures or the sounds mixed up.

Afterwards, the cameras and microphones will be off to other places – perhaps to Horse Trials or the the General Assembly. Cameras will take pictures of *anything*, ugly or beautiful. Microphones will pick up *anything*, true or false. It just depends where you point them.

We all have two little cameras – one behind each eye. They too will look at anything we put in front of them – ugly or beautiful, pleasant or horrid. In our ears we all have microphones which can pick up lies or truth, happy things or sad. And what about the broadcasting set? That's our mouth. With it we can broadcast truth or lies, kind words or cruel.

There's only one way of making sure that we see no evil, hear no evil and speak no evil, and that is to ask Jesus to control and guide our hearing and seeing and speaking.

He will help us to guard our lips from evil and our tongues from speaking lies.

——————————— · ———————————

We need some power

The other day two great big men arrived at the Manse to drill some holes in the stonework of the garage, to prepare for new doors to be put on. Before they began, they came to the study window and very politely asked, "Can you help us?" I wasn't too sure how good I would be at boring holes in a stone wall, so I was a bit doubtful, especially when they said, "We'd like some power." I looked at their muscles and felt mine and thought, "Anything they can do, I can do – a lot worse." Then they handed me a bit of flex and said, "Just plug it in." I could manage that. Then I saw that they had a huge Black & Decker drill. When I switched on the power the drill began to go through the stone as if it were butter.

Although you and I may not have much strength or cleverness

in ourselves, we can always draw upon the strength and goodness of God, and so help people far wiser and stronger than we are ourselves.

That is why we pray, and we can all do that, whether we are young or old, clever or not so clever, sick or healthy.

Every time we pray for others, we make a connection for them with the love and wisdom, with the power and pity of God.

That is why men and women, and boys and girls, ought to pray.

The car key

The other day I had to go to Glasgow and I went by car. All went well on the way down, but when I was ready to come home, I had the most awful problem. It was not that there was anything wrong with the car – it was in fine running order. I didn't have a flat tyre. I had lots of petrol in the tank. It was just that I couldn't get into it. Now, you might think that I had left the ignition key in the ignition and had locked the car door, but I'm not as daft as that. No. The ignition key was in my pocket – in my coat pocket. The *coat* was locked in the car – and it took two police cars, five policemen, three janitors and the helpful advice of twenty-nine assorted passers-by before the door was finally opened.

A car key is only a little thing, but it opens up the way to all the power that is hidden in the engine.

Prayer too seems such a small, unimportant thing. Yet it opens the way to the heart of God and makes free to us his mighty power to help. We need that help every day we live, from the time we're very young till we're quite, quite old. We need God's help if we're to live life as it was meant to be lived – after the pattern of Christ.

God-made

Men are able to make very wonderful things these days. Among the most exciting are the spaceships which rush at terrific speed millions of miles up into space. A while ago there was one which had two monkeys as passengers. It is marvellous what scientists and engineers can make, isn't it? But it is worth remembering that there are some things we men cannot make. We can make the spaceships, but we cannot make the men to go into them. We cannot even make the monkeys. Indeed, if all the manufacturers and all the scientists in the world got together they could not make even one single little flower – not even a daisy. Only God can make a daisy, or a monkey, or a man. Every living thing has come from his hands.

When your mother buys something in the shops, if she is wise, she very often looks to see where it is made. Most articles are stamped "Made in Great Britain" or "Made in Canada", or wherever it may be. Some things, especially souvenirs from holiday places, are stamped with a picture of the place where they come from – Isle of Man, London, Paris, as the case may be.

Every boy and girl born into the world is clearly marked "Made by God", and there is a picture of God stamped on each one. Sometimes it may be a little rubbed or dirty or obscured, but always it is there on every one – the image of God.

That is why we should not waste our lives in silly or wicked ways. We are made by God for wonderful things, for his service. We should not waste this life which God has given, and which Christ has redeemed, in selfish idleness. "Ye are not your own," as St. Paul said to the Corinthians, "ye are bought with a price." "The Lord he is God: it is he that hath made us and not we ourselves." *(Psalm 100.3)*

SNEEZES AND WHEEZES

Your own temperature

The other day a boy I know thought he would have a day off school so he said he didn't feel well. He looked well enough, but, just to make sure, his mother let him stay in bed for a little, gave him a hot-water bottle and said "We'll take your temperature." She gave him the thermometer and told him to put it in his armpit, and then she went away and did something else. Presently, she came back and took the thermometer from a patient who looked very healthy, but curiously confident that he would not not be going to school. When she looked at the thermometer, the mother got a shock, for it registered 106°! If ever your temperature is as high as that, you will be very, very ill indeed. But this particular mother, being a very wise woman, looked at the boy again. She shook the thermometer down and gave it back to him and said, "Now we will take that temperature again, but first give me the hot-water bottle." Yes, you have guessed it. The bad boy had taken the temperature of the hot-water bottle instead of his own. I hope none of your parents are going to be cross with me for passing on the tip, for there is not much sense in taking the temperature of the hot-water bottle. It is your own temperature that matters.

In the same way, there is not much sense in getting your parents to do your homework or in copying someone else's work at school. It is *your own* work that matters. Nor can we leave it to someone else to say our prayers or to go to church. We must be able to speak, as the Psalmist does, of "our own God." *(Psalm 67.8).*

———————— · ————————

The cold

I had something this week. I didn't want it but I didn't want to give it away to anybody. Finally I gave it to my wife. She didn't want it either, but she took it. Now we've both got it and we wish we could get rid of it, but don't want to give it to anyone else. Here's a hint. If you don't keep your distance you'll get it too.

Some things we should share, like our sweets and our happiness. But other things we are far better to keep to ourselves, like a cold, or bad temper, or a cruel story about anyone, or anything unclean.

Don't listen to these bad things if you can help it. But if you hear them don't pass them on, in imitation of Jesus who, as St. Peter tells us, never sinned nor told a lie.

The sneeze

Yesterday when I was at a meeting, I suddenly sneezed. I got my hanky out in time, but even so I could see the people round about me edging away, thinking "Maybe Mr. Gray has flu. If we don't watch out we might get it too, for flu is very infectious."

The word flu is short for influenza, and influenza is simply the Italian word for "influence". Influenza was called influenza just because it was so easy to pass it on to others.

Other things besides illness are easy to pass on – misery or laughter, truth, or falsehood, kindness or cruelty. That is why you should choose your friends very carefully, for your friends will influence you for good or bad.

Above all, seek the friendship of Christ and think much of him. He will influence you, and only for good. When people met the first Christians, we read in *Acts 4.13* that "they recognized them (Peter and John) as companions of Jesus."

It would be wonderful if people looking at us could tell right away, by our kindness, our courage, our good temper, that you and I had been much in the company of Jesus.

——————— · ———————

The sore throat

Can you hear me, girls and boys? Raise your hands if you can hear me. It is not very easy to speak to you all when I have a sore throat. In fact it is not very easy to speak to you all at any time.

How terrible it must be when you have something to say to the whole world. God wanted to speak to everybody in the world and even God did not find it easy. Your first book was a picture book. God tried to say what he had to say in lovely pictures, so he made the world very beautiful. He made spring, summer, autumn and winter. He made flowers and fruit and birds and animals. Some people noticed all the loveliness and thought of God, but most people took all the beauty for granted.

God tried whispering to the world. That's what we call "conscience", when God whispers deep down in our hearts, but people made so much noise that they did not hear conscience.

Then God thought he'd send special messengers. We call them "prophets". They said "Hear the word of the Lord," and then they said what God had told them to say, but people did not listen. Mostly they paid no attention to the prophets. Sometimes they killed them.

Finally God saw that there was only one way to speak to everybody in all the world, through all the centuries. He decided to send his own son. And in Christ, God's word became flesh.

We're always glad to get a message from a friend. Part of the reason why we are happy at Christmas is because we get so many cards and letters from friends. But the best Christmas message is the one that comes from God, the friend of us all. The message is this, that God loves us all just as if there were only one of us to love.

God loves you. This is the good tiding of great joy which shall be to all people.

The final certificate

Some time ago I was ill in bed for two or three weeks and the doctor came to see me on several occasions. One day he came as usual, took my pulse and temperature, and did all the usual things that doctors do, and then he said a strange thing, "I think I will give you a 'Final Certificate'."

Well! Immediately there flashed into my mind thoughts of the Cup Final, the Final Edition of a paper, Final Examinations. I thought to myself, "This is frightful. It means the end." I must have looked a little unhappy, for the doctor said, "I will sign you off." That seemed even worse. "Will that be the end of me?" I asked. "No," he replied, laughingly, "it is the end of your illness." As I had been feeling a lot better, I knew he was right.

One of the few good things about illness is that, like everything else that is unpleasant, it has to end. Of course, nice things end too – ice-cream ends very quickly, and parties, and holidays – even life itself. But if we love and trust the Lord Jesus there shall be no end for us of the very nicest things of all, no end of beauty, no end of joy, no end of love or of life itself. For we have been given a wonderful promise about Christ, "of his kingdom there shall be no end." *(Luke 1.33).*

It's infectious

One day when we were in America we meant to go to a rodeo. We had just got to Oklahoma where there are usually lots of rodeos and we were looking forward to seeing wild horses being broken and all the other exciting things which happen at rodeos.

But all the rodeos had been cancelled because a mysterious and deadly disease had broken out among the horses, and this disease, like many other diseases among horses and people, was "catching" – what doctors call "infectious". It passes easily from one person or animal to another.

That's true of so many other evil things – bad temper, lies, dishonesty. But it is also true of some of the nicest things – kindness is infectious, and cheerfulness, and so is the love of God and of his son Jesus. If we truly love God and show it by the way we speak and live, others will catch Christianity from us.

That is how the Church grew at first. That is how it grows still. Here is one way in which we can all help the Church, and the world, and God, by letting others catch faith in God from us. It is something like that Jesus meant when he said "You will be witnesses to me through all the world." *(Acts 1.8)*

GOD'S WONDERFUL WORLD

Something worth singing about

Would you like to hear a better song than . . . (whatever is number one at the moment) and a better singer than . . . (whoever is the favourite of the moment)? Well, you can. All you have to do is to get up really early tomorrow and you'll hear the dawn chorus of the birds. We're lucky here for we have a lot of birds and a great number of different kinds.

There is never any difficulty in telling one bird from another, for every bird has its own song and it sticks to it.

"COOOK, COOOK, COOOK" says the dove.

"CAW, CAW, CAW" says the rook.

"CHIRP, CHIRP, CHIRP" sings the sparrow.

"TSI, TSI, TSI, CHINK" is the call of the tit.

"CHICK, CHOOK, CHOOK, CHOOK" says the thrush.

"CH, CH, CH, CH, CH" says the chaffinch.

They never seem to grow tired of singing their own song over and over again. Why should they? Some things are worth singing and saying over and over again. In the Book of Psalms, in the last psalm the word "praise" is used twice in every verse. In Psalm 136 there are twenty-six verses, and in each verse come the words, "O give thanks unto the Lord, for his mercy endures for ever."

Don't always be looking for a new song. If you know something worth singing, or worth saying, sing or say it over and over again.

———————— · ————————

The greatest miracle of all

Do you know what a miracle is, boys and girls? Something absolutely marvellous.

Would you like to see a miracle right here in the Cathedral? Now? Are you all ready? Well, turn your head to the left. Now to the right. Now look ahead. Now turn round and look behind you. Now try to see as much of yourself as you can see. What do you see? Just a man or woman, a boy or a girl. Nothing wonderful in that, you say. Oh, but there is. There is no greater miracle than a human being like you or me.

Think of your brain – ten thousand million nerve cells in your head. Although some people's brain cells seem to work harder than others, even those which do not work very well are marvellous. Nobody could make a machine with ten thousand million moving parts – except God.

Or think of your nose – it can smell about fifty thousand different smells.

Or your heart. It beats seventy-two times every minute, four thousand, three hundred and twenty times an hour, over one hundred thousand times a day, about thirty-five million times a year.

Every one of us is a miracle whom only God could have made.

The most wonderful thing about us is not our hearts, nor our heads, nor our whole bodies, but this – that we are made like God, that we are able to speak to him in prayer, and to know he is always near us in love.

That is what the Bible means when it says that God made us in his own likeness.

Window-boxes

Have you ever been to Switzerland? Last week I was in Lucerne, which is one of the most beautiful towns in Switzerland, and maybe in the world. Part of what makes it so beautiful is the fact that on every window-sill, on the banks and the railway station, on hotels and people's houses, there are window-boxes full of flowers, mostly scarlet geraniums and pink and purple petunias. Now, the flowers are not provided by the government or by the town. Each house, each shop, each office provides its own and looks after its own. So everywhere one looks there are these wonderful flowers.

That is how anything good or useful is done – by a great number of people each doing their share. There are eight thousand of us in Dunblane. If each of us tried hard to bring some beauty, some goodness, some happiness into the world, what a difference it would make to Dunblane, and to Scotland, and to the world. If eight thousand of us smiled an extra smile a day, that would be fifty-six thousand every week, nearly half a million every year! If each of us said even one extra pleasant thing a day or did one extra kindness, that would mean nearly half a million extra kindnesses a year. What a difference that would make!

This is the way, the only way, in which God's work will be done in the world – not by one or two great people, but by every one of us doing what we can for God, who has done so much for us. It was something like this Jesus meant when he said "Your light must shine before people." *(Matthew 5.16)*

———————— · ————————

Tree roots

Boys and girls, a short time ago, I was walking through a forest. It was a forest of pine trees, which are like giant Christmas trees. At one point I came across a tree which had fallen down. The roots which normally lay under the ground were standing upright and the huge tree was lying along the ground.

This tree had been blown down in a storm. The reason why the tree had been blown down was because its roots had not grown deep into the soil. The roots were there, but they had grown out and out from the trunk, but just under the soil. The roots had nothing to grip on to. So when the wind blew strongly the tree could not stand up to it and it fell over. You know, boys and girls, we have to get a grip of something in life if we are not to be blown over by the storms of life. The surest and best thing to hold on to in life is God's love for each of us. God showed his love towards us in sending Jesus to die on the cross for us. If we hold on to that truth then, when the storms of life come, when we are blown about by the troubles of life, then we will be able to stand up straight like a tree which has deep roots.

That is what St. Paul meant when he said that we should be rooted and grounded in love.

The camel

You know what a camel is, girls and boys, don't you? It's like a horse with a funny face and one or two humps. Well, once upon a time a man was crossing the desert on his camel. It was rather a special camel for it could talk. Night came on and the man decided to go to bed. He set up his little tent and got into it and settled down to sleep. The camel lay down outside. For a little while there was peace, and then the camel said, "Master, it is very cold out here. The tip of my nose is frozen. Could I just put the tip of my nose into your tent?" Well, the man was a very kind man so he said to the camel, "Of course, put your poor cold nose into the tent." So the man settled down again to sleep. He had just dropped off when the camel said, "Master?" A little crossly the man said, "What is it now?" The camel said, "Master, my nose is warm but my ears are frozen. Surely there would be room for my head in the tent." "Oh, all right" said the man, and into the tent came the camel's head.

For a while all was peace again until the camel said, "Master, my forelegs are so cold that I won't be able to walk tomorrow." Well, things were beginning to become a bit crowded in the tent, but the man, with the camel's head just beside him, could hardly refuse.

Then the camel said, "It's silly to have my forelegs in the tent and my hindlegs outside." So, before long, the whole camel was in the tent and, as he filled it all up, the poor man was outside in the cold. You may be sure that the next time that the camel asked just to get his nose into the tent, he would be told "No" *very* firmly. That's the story, and what we should learn from it is not to let any bad thing get even its nose into our lives. It may not seem very bad to tell a little lie, but if you once tell one it won't be long before you are telling great big whoppers. To steal a chocolate from the bottom layer in the box may not seem a big sin, but if you begin to steal you'll find it hard to stop.

Don't let any kind of cruel or nasty or dishonest thing get into your minds or your lives, and then nothing bad will get the chance to grow. The best way to keep the bad things out is to fill your minds and lives with good things, to learn about Jesus and so think about him. Then there won't be room in your minds or hearts for even the tip of the nose of anything cruel or nasty or dishonest.

The apple seed

Do you know what I have here, boys and girls? It is a seed from an apple. It is so small you can hardly see it, but if you plant it and look after it very carefully, it will grow into a little tree. Then, after some years, it will be a great tree and bear apples itself – and will save you from coming into the Manse garden to steal mine!

Many things that are now big were once very little. Once upon a time there was a very small church where this one now stands. After a time that church became too small and another larger church was built. I'm sure the good men who built the first tiny church would not have believed that this great church would one day replace it but:

> "Large streams from little fountains flow
> Tall oaks from little acorns grow."

That is why it is important to learn your lessons at school. That is why it is important to learn good habits, habits of truthfulness and kindliness and cheerfulness, at the very beginning of your lives. That is why it is important above all to learn about Jesus and begin, just begin, to let him have his way with you.

As one of the prophets in the Old Testament said, "Don't despise small things." *(Zechariah 5.10)*

Greedy monkey

Have you ever been to the zoo, girls and boys? If you have, I'm sure you spent a good deal of time in the monkey house. They are fascinating little beasts, so quick and clever.

I used to wonder how people ever managed to catch them. The

other day I read how it is done, or at least how it is done in one part of South Africa.

You know what a pumpkin is, don't you? It is a bit like a very large melon. Cinderella's coach was made, if you remember, out of a pumpkin. Apparently monkeys are very fond of pumpkin seeds. So when they want to catch one, the hunters take a nice big pumpkin and make a hole in the skin, big enough for a monkey's paw to get through, but no bigger. They leave it outdoors. In the middle of the night the monkey comes and looks all round about and makes sure that nobody is near. Then he thrusts his paw into the pumpkin and takes a handful of seed and pulls his paw out – or tries to! But his paw won't fit through the hole now that it's full of seeds. Apparently, once he has grasped the seeds he is too greedy to let go and so, in the morning, he is made a prisoner and spends the rest of his life in captivity.

You know, that is what can happen to people too. If we are selfish and grasping we become prisoners to our own greed. If you and I keep on trying to get more and more for ourselves, and give less and less to others, our lives become mean and poor and narrow. The only real way to live is to follow Christ who just gave and gave all the time, seeking nothing for himself, and finally he even gave himself.

It was Jesus himself who said, "It is more blessed to give than to receive " – more fun to give than to get. *(Acts 20.35)*

Conkers

I got a present yesterday which I'm going to divide with you all after the service – it is a great big bag of the finest conkers you ever saw.

Do you know how to win in a game of conkers? You can steep your conker in vinegar. They say that makes it hard. But the best tip is to hold the string of your conker *very* tight when you're hitting another conker, but when someone is hitting yours, you must hold the string very loosely and let it slip in your hand.

You'll beat anybody that way – anybody, that is, except one person, and that's yourself. For you see, you know your own tricks and can dodge your own most determined blows. You can't ever win in the battle with yourself. You can't win in the fight with your own selfishness, your own laziness, your own bad temper and greed. For you know all your own mean tricks.

In the battle with self you can't win – by yourself – but God can win for you. If you ask him to, and really mean it, he'll come into your life and defeat all the temptations which have been defeating you. That is what St. Paul meant when he said, "We are more then conquerors through Christ who loves us." *(Romans 8.37)*

Honesty

In my hand, boys and girls, I have quite a number of seeds. There will be one for each of you after the service. If you plant your seed in the garden or in a pot, then, after a while, you should have a fine plant which has a nice little purple flower. But the interesting thing about this particular plant is not so much the flower, as the seed pods. They are like the pods of peas or beans except for one thing – these seed pods have little windows in them so you can see through to the seeds inside. I think that may be where the plant gets its name from – there is nothing hidden in it, you can see right through it. What is it called? Yes! It is Honesty. It has nothing to hide.

That is a good way for a plant to grow, and a good way for a boy or a girl to grow, with nothing to hide. It is also a good way for a man or a woman to live – within nothing deceitful, nothing underhand, nothing dishonest, nothing secretive in their hearts or lives.

But there's something else, boys and girls. Every Honesty plant, however big it may become, begins as a tiny little seed. Many good things in the world or in our lives begin as something very small.

So, when you plant your Honesty seed today in your garden or indoors, plant a seed of goodness in the world. Do something this very day, however little, to please Christ – be pleasant to someone disagreeable, write a letter to someone who'll be pleased to receive it, give a present to someone who does not expect it, go and see an old person who is lonely – but *make a beginning*. Plant some little seed of kindness or honesty, of truth or love in the world.

God is wonderfully generous. He helps the seeds we plant in the earth and the seeds of goodness we plant in the world to grow; and he helps every seed of honesty and goodness we welcome in our hearts to grow in our lives.

Jesus once said, "The Kingdom of Heaven is like a man who sowed good seed." *(Matthew 13.24)*

The log of wood

I don't have a story for you this morning, boys and girls, but I have brought along a friend to tell a story for me. It's not another minister. It is a log of wood. It doesn't look a very clever log of wood, but it is wonderful what you can learn from it. For example, the kind of bark on the outside tells you the name of the tree. It is called an ash. Then, if you look at the end, you'll find that there are a whole lot of rings, one inside the other. Each ring takes a year to grow – this particular log has twenty-one rings. A tree doesn't show rings until it is five years old, so that tells you that the tree was twenty-six years old when it was cut down. Some of the rings are broader than others, and that tells you that in that particular year there was more rain than usual. If you know a lot about trees and look very carefully, you can tell if this tree grew up on a hill or down in a valley. You can even tell what direction the wind usually came from.

Every tree carries in itself the story of its own life, and so do we all. Everything we learn, everything that we do, everything that happens to us leaves marks on us – on our minds, on our hearts and even on the lines on our faces.

All the time, every day, like the trees, we are all growing. If, as we grow, we try to follow Jesus, then like the rings on the trees we shall show in our lives the love and gentleness, the truth and goodness which are the marks of those who belong to him.

——————— · ———————

The Bible Zoo

You all know what a zoo is, boys and girls – a place where we may see wild animals and birds and fish in as near natural conditions as possible – you may have been to the zoo in Edinburgh or Glasgow. One zoo is pretty much the same as the next.

There's one zoo I'd very much like to visit. It is in Jerusalem and it is a Bible Zoo. In it all the birds and beasts and fish mentioned in the Bible are kept. Each has a label with its proper name and the chapter and verse where it is found in the Bible. I wonder how many you could think of?

There's the lion which Samson slew; there's the sparrow which made her nest in the temple; there's the snake from the Garden of Eden; there are the pigs which rushed down the hill to the sea in Gadara; there is the camel the man swallowed who would not swallow the gnat; there are the sheep the shepherds were watching when Jesus came. There would have been the fatted calf

– but it had been eaten! There are the doves which were bought and sold in the temple. There is the cock which crew to remind Peter of his betrayal of Jesus.

Do you know which animal I think should have the place of honour? The donkey. Why? Because it was on a donkey that Jesus rode into Jerusalem to die for us all.

A donkey is not a very big beast, nor a very fierce one, nor a very handsome one, but Jesus our Lord was ready to use him.

Just as Jesus was ready to use an ordinary little donkey, he will use us if we ask him to, to help and heal and serve other people and to serve him in the world for which he died.

The Safari Park comes to town

Have you ever been to a Safari Park? I've been just once, but sometimes in the playground at school or even outside the Sunday School or the Junior Choir I wonder if the Safari Park has come to Dunblane, for this is what I hear:

"You're a clumsy big elephant." "You're a lazy dog." "You're a mean cat." "You're a cheeky monkey." "You've got the brain of a hen." "You're as slow as a tortoise."

We're very hard on the poor animals, blaming them for having all our faults. I wonder if they say anything to each other about us – if the cow says to the calf "You're as greedy as a boy," or if the cat says to the kitten "You're as untidy as a girl," or if all the animals say "Don't be so human" where we say "Don't be so beastly." We shouldn't treat animals so badly nor say nasty things about them. In particular we should never say "You're a stupid donkey," for Jesus, who loved all animals, had, I think, a special love for donkeys. It was on a donkey that his parents took him into Egypt when he was a baby and it was on a donkey that he came into Jerusalem on the first Palm Sunday to die for us all.

Don't despise the donkey or any of God's creatures, for God does not despise them any more than he despises you and me.

St. Paul tells us that God has specially chosen things that people despise for his own wonderful purposes: "God chose what the world looks down on and despises." *(1st Corinthians 1.28)*

———————— · ————————

The wasps' nest

Girls and boys, I often have things in the pulpit to show you. This morning you will hardly believe what I have here with me. It is a house. It is not a doll's house. It is a house which has really been lived in and it has hundreds of rooms. Of course, they're not very big rooms, but they are all perfect and they are all the same size and shape. This particular house was found the other day in the loft of the Manse. Do you want to see it? I wonder if any of you can tell me who used to live in this house with its hundreds of rooms. I'll give you a hint. If they were still living in it I wouldn't go near it. It's a wasps' nest.

It is wonderful how these clever little insects strip the bark off trees and build their little houses where they have their babies and bring them up year after year.

Grown-ups often make a great fuss about the kind of house they live in, or the sort of clothes they wear, or the food they eat – and sometimes children do too. We shouldn't. We really shouldn't worry so much about things.

Jesus once said "Look at the birds. Think of the flowers. God who has looked after them will look after us too." He made us and loves us, just as he made and just as he loves the flowers, the birds and the beasts – even the wasps.

———————— · ————————

The half horse

There's a girl I know called Alison. One day she came to her mother and said "Mummy, there's half a horse on the pavement." Her mother got a great shock – she thought there must have been a dreadful accident and that the poor horse had been killed. Out she rushed, but all she found was a perfectly ordinary, healthy horse, drawing a milk van. Attracted by some fresh grass it had moved over so that its front hooves were on the pavement while its hind legs were still on the road. Everybody laughed and told Alison that she should have said that there was a horse half on the pavement, not that there was a half horse on the pavement. You can't have half a horse any more than you can have a half boy or a half girl.

We all know that, but often we forget and give only half of ourselves, half of our minds or half of our attention, to what we are doing, and that is where we go wrong. You can't watch television *and* do your homework. You can't whisper to your neighbour *and* listen to the children's talk. You can only make a good job of things if you put your whole heart and soul into whatever you happen to be doing, whether it is reading or playing a game or saying your prayers.

When you dance the Hokey-Cokey, you first of all put your right hand in, then your left hand, then your right foot, then your left foot and so on, but finally you've got to put your whole self in.

When Jesus asks you to be his servant, he doesn't just want your right hand or your left, your head or your feet. He wants your whole self to be his.

Crows

Boys and girls, just to the left as you leave the churchyard there is a rubbish basket attached to a lamp-post. One day I was very cross to see all the waste-paper and rubbish tipped out on to the pavement. Our beadle knows most things about the village so I went and asked him if he knew who the wicked person was who had made such a mess. He knew of course, and he told me. It wasn't a man, it wasn't a woman, it wasn't a boy and it wasn't a girl. Who do you think was to blame? It was – a crow! Apparently crows like to eat fish and chips on a Friday or Saturday night, so they go through the bins for what they can find. Well, it's very clever of the crows to find a free fish supper and nobody would mind if only they'd put all the papers and bags back into the rubbish basket when they're finished. But they're not clever enough for that. Even the stupidest crow in the world can make a mess. Even the cleverest crow in the world can't clear it up.

It is so much easier for crows – or for people – to spoil things than to put them right, so much easier to hurt than to heal.

Once you have said something that isn't true you can't unsay it. Once you have done something wrong it is very hard to undo the harm you've done.

But Christ our Lord will help us, if we ask him, not to say or do the wrong or hurtful things which we can't put right. That is what we're asking him to do when we say the Lord's Prayer, "Lead us not into temptation, but deliver us from evil." If we say the prayer and really mean it, he will always answer it and help us.

———————— · ————————

The Manse garden

Girls and boys, I have a friend who is a minister, and he's a very good minister. He is a good preacher. He's a good visitor. He's good with old folk. He is good with young people. But . . . (it's a pity there has to be a "but", but there always is). Well, my friend is a good minister in every way, but he's a terrible gardener. His Manse garden is a disgrace. He can't even grow grass. The lawn is all burnt and patchy, and the only things he can grow are weeds.

Well, one of the elders took the minister aside and gave him the names of two chemicals, chemical A to make the lawn grow and chemical B to kill the weeds. So the minister went off to the town and bought some chemical A to make the lawn grow and chemical B to kill the weeds. But . . . (there's always a "but"). But he got them mixed up. He put chemical B on the lawn and chemical A on the paths. Now all the grass on the lawn is dead and the weeds on the path are about four feet high and still growing. Pity the poor minister.

But, you know, boys and girls and grown-ups often do the same thing. We encourage bad habits and make them grow like weeds in our lives. We waste time and effort and money in silly ways. We don't cultivate good habits like obedience, honesty, courtesy, kindliness, nor the most important of all habits like worshipping God, reading our Bible and saying our prayers.

If we want to be like Jesus it doesn't just happen. We've got to make some effort. It was something like that St. Paul meant when he said "Love earnestly the best gifts."

———————— · ————————

More about the Manse garden

(Taraxacum Dens Leonis)

You know the Manse garden, girls and boys. It is a very interesting garden with all sorts of interesting things in it. We've had hedgehogs, squirrels, a hare, a mole, a rabbit and lots and lots

of birds, as well as Mrs. Gray and a few boys and me. It's quite a
menagerie. Just this last week or two there have been dozens of
things with a long name. They are called *Taraxacum Dens Leonis*.
They sound very fierce and terrible but I've brought one with me.
I'll try to make sure it doesn't bite any of you or chase the Junior
Choir.

Do you want to see a real *Taraxacum Dens Leonis*? Well, here it
is. It's just a plain ordinary dandelion. "Dandelion" is just the way
we pronounce the French words "Dent de lion", which means
Lion's Tooth. The leaf is said to look like a lion's tooth.

Lots of flowers have special Latin names as well as everyday
ones. The little forget-me-not is called *Myosotis*. A *Bellis Perennis*
is the common daisy and a *Galanthus Nivalis* is a snowdrop.

It is much better to have a name that gives a kind of picture like
dandelion or snowdrop, than to have a grand name that does not
really suit.

You and I are called "Christians". Is it a good name for us, do
you think? Are we "like Christ" even a little bit? Do we speak and
act like Christ? Do we want to be more like Christ?

If you and I do want to be more like him and if we ask him to,
he'll help us to grow every day in goodness and in likeness to
himself – so we'll have the right to be called "Christians" –
Christ's folk. Christ's followers. Christ's friends.

———————— · ————————

The Manse garden again

(Sarcoptis)

Have you ever been to a Safari Park? If you haven't, then you
could save money by coming to the Manse garden instead. We
don't charge an admission fee and we've lots of wild beasts there. I
know. This week I've been bitten by two of them.

One was called a *Sarcoptis*. It sounds a very savage animal, and it was too, but it wasn't very big. In fact it was so small that I couldn't see it, but it was there, just the same. I've got the lumps to prove it. *Sarcoptis* is its fancy name. Its ordinary name is a berry bug. What your father calls it I don't know!

We've larger wild animals in the Manse garden too. They're called *Cheronomidae Ceratopogon*. Their other name is the midge. The Red Indians in America have a name for all these tiny beasts that bite. They call them "No-see-ums" and that's a very good name for them, for though you feel them, you don't see them. It's better to use a name that fits rather than a long fancy name which nobody understands.

We're told in the bible that it was a town called Antioch that the followers of Jesus were first called Christians. People felt it was a good name for them, for they followed so closely in the footsteps of Christ that they had become like him.

I wonder if that is a good name for us. It will only be if we try to be like Christ and to follow where he leads.

Pruning shears

Do you like flowers? So do I. Which flowers do you like best? Roses. So do I. But if you are going to learn to grow roses, you'll have to learn to use something very ugly which I'm going to show you – pruning shears. If you want to have lots of lovely roses when June comes, you'll have to prune the rose bushes. That just means cutting away all the dead wood and all the unnecessary shoots to give the new growth a chance. It is funny when you think that to make a bush grow better you have to cut lots of it away. But that is how it is with roses.

And that is how it is with life. If your life is to be fine and good you've got to prune it by cutting out all the silly, lazy, ugly and evil things so that the things which are good and wise and lovely may flourish and grow.

Sometimes when you are pruning roses it is hard to know which branches to cut and which to leave. Christ knows all about growing things, and he knows all about people. If we let him have his way with us he will cut out from all our lives everything which hinders or prevent us from growing more like him every day. And to be like Christ is to be the best that we can be.

1 *Poor pelican*

Do you know what a pelican is, boys and girls? It is a bird with a very large beak. Like many other creatures with big mouths, it is rather a silly sort of bird. David Livingstone in his diary tells of something the pelican does which shows how silly it is.

The pelican, it seems, likes to eat fish, and it is rather good at catching them, perhaps because the fish are even more stupid than it is itself. Now, in Africa there is another bird called the fish-hawk. As its name shows, it also is fond of fish, but is much too lazy to catch them for itself. What the fish-hawk does is this. It watches till a pelican has a nice, big fish in its bill and then it comes swooping down from the sky, making the most fiendish and horrible cries. Every time the pelican hears the fish-hawk it does the same thing. It opens its big mouth in wonder and looks up to see where all the noise is coming from. The fish-hawk then neatly snatches the fish out of the pelican's mouth and goes off somewhere for a nice meal. This has been going on for thousands of years. The pelican catches the fish. The fish-hawk screams. The pelican opens its bill and looks up and – off with the fish darts the fish-hawk. One would expect the pelican to learn its lesson in time, learn to pay no attention to the screaming of its enemy, or at least learn not to open its mouth. Apparently each time the poor, silly pelican forgets.

Some people would say that the lesson of this story is simply, "Keep your mouth shut." Mostly, that is good advice. But there is a better lesson and it is this. If you have something which is good and useful, hold on to it and do not let it go, even if noisy people are screaming at you to do so. If you have a rule not to swear, or lie, or cheat, or miss church, or forget your prayers or your reading of the Bible, then stick to your rule no matter what anybody may say. Hold on to your good resolution even though people may make fun of you or try to hurt you for it. It was something like this that St. Paul meant when he said to the Christians at Thessalonica – "Hold fast to that which is good." *(1 Thessalonians 5.21)*

The bean that grew

You will all have read the story of Jack and the Beanstalk when you were little, but have you ever tried to grow a beanstalk of your own? You can, you know, even if you live in a house which has no garden. All you must do is to wait until your mother is not too busy and then ask her for an ordinary white butter bean, a glass jamjar, a little bit of cotton-wool and some old blotting-paper. Line the jar with the blotting-paper and fill the centre with loosely-packed cotton-wool. Place the bean, or two beans if you can get them, between the blotting-paper and the side of the jar, then dampen the cotton wool and leave the jar near a window. In a day or two the bean will grow roots and in a very few weeks you will have a fine beanstalk, all because you treated the bean in the right way. The other beans in the cupboard in the kitchen will still be the same hard little things they always were. Only the one which is treated properly will grow.

The same is true of boys and girls. If they are to grow up strong, tall and clever, they must get lots of fresh air and sunshine, plenty of good food and sleep. And the same is true of growing in goodness. That will happen only to those who worship God regularly, and pray, and are ready to learn about Jesus whom he has sent. Only so will we do what St. Peter hoped we would do, "Grow in grace, and in the knowledge of our Lord and Saviour Jesus Christ." *(2 Peter 3.18)*

-------------------- · --------------------

The sweetpea chancel

In the Borders of Scotland and England there is a lovely parish called Sprowston, and in the middle of the parish there is a little parish church.

In 1911, the minister of the parish was the Reverend Denholm Frazer. At that time the church was just a very plain oblong building. The minister thought the church would look much nicer if it had a little chancel for the Communion Table to stand in. When he found out how much it would cost, however, he felt very depressed, because it was a lot of money and the people of Sprowston did not have very much money.

When Mr. Frazer wasn't visiting or preaching, he used to work in his garden. He liked growing flowers best, and most of all he liked to grow sweetpeas. One day a friend came in with a copy of the *Daily Mail* in which there was news of a competition for the best sweetpeas in Great Britain. The friend told Mr. Frazer that he should enter. The minister laughed. He didn't think he could possibly win the competition, since there would be so many very clever, professional gardeners near London competing. However, he was persuaded to have a try. Finally, he sent two bunches all the way to London.

But he wasn't the only gardener who thought he'd have a try. There were no fewer than thirty-eight thousand bunches of sweetpeas from all over Britain! No names were on the flowers –

just numbers. The judges worked away and after a few days they had chosen the three best bunches. The first would get a prize of £1,000, the second £100 and the third £50. When they opened the numbered envelopes which contained the names of the competitors, they discovered that the first and the third had come from Sprowston Manse. A telegram was sent off, telling Mr. Frazer of his win. When the postmistress delivered it, she was so excited that she fell down in a faint!

So now the minister had £1,050 and he was able to go ahead and build a lovely little chancel – the only chancel in the world, you might say, built out of sweetpeas. Any time you're in Sprowston, go into the church. You'll see the chancel and the Communion Table, and on it, if they're in season, a bowl of sweetpeas.

And the moral of this story is a very simple one. If you do what you can do, and do it as well as you can, the Lord will provide in a marvellous way all you really need.

———————— · ————————

sᴵ ʒ. ✓ *The new planet*

Have you seen any good planets lately, boys and girls? You have, you know. There is one you all know very well. The Earth is a planet – a great material ball which wanders round the sun. The other planets are Mercury, Venus, Mars, Jupiter, Saturn, Uranus, Neptune and Pluto. That makes nine, including the Earth. But it seems that even planets are going decimal, for recently some American scientists announced that they were quite sure that there was a tenth planet. Although it is huge, far, far bigger than the Earth, no one has yet seen it. "Well," you may ask, "what makes the scientists think that it exists at all, if nobody has ever seen it?" It appears that these clever men have, for a time, been watching very carefully the behaviour of other planets and of comets like the famous Halley's Comet which appears every seventy-six years. They have worked out by means of computers that, although they cannot see it, this new planet *must* be there. They have even decided its probable size and how long it takes to go round the sun.

Just in the same way, although none of us has ever seen God, we can be sure that he is there. If you look at the beauty of the world, even of a single flower, it is obvious that it must have been made by someone to whom beauty meant a great deal. If you look into the eyes of someone who loves you dearly, like your mother, you can be pretty sure that there is a God who has given us each other to love. Above all, if by reading the gospels you come to know Jesus Christ, you begin to be very sure of God, though you have never seen him. That, I think, is what St. John meant when he said, "No man hath seen God at any time; the only begotten Son, which is in the bosom of the Father, he hath declared him." *(John 1.18)*

The mouse

Do you know what an artist is? Someone who can draw or paint. Well, artists have to eat like other people, and in order to eat they have to have money. To obtain money they have to sell their drawings and paintings.

A long time ago, there lived in America an artist who just couldn't sell his drawings. No matter what he drew, people didn't seem to want to buy. One day he was feeling very discouraged. As he sat very quietly, a little mouse crept out of its hole and ran about picking up some crumbs he had dropped. As he watched it, the artist drew one picture of the mouse and then another and another. Very soon he sold some of the drawings of the mouse, and then more and more. The little mouse appeared in comic strips, and then on films, and then on television, until almost everybody in the world knew the artist, Walt Disney, and his little friend the mouse, for that little friend was none other than Mickey Mouse.

You know, I think our Lord Jesus Christ, who did not even look down on a little donkey, would have enjoyed Mickey Mouse. God himself likes to use weak and foolish things for his own good purposes, God is willing to use you and me.

The acorn

Girls and boys, I want you to have a look at the pews on which you are sitting and at the book boards in front of you. They're made of wood, of a very special type of wood. What kind of wood is it? It's a three-letter word. It's oak. That's the wood they made ships out of in the old days, and fine sturdy tables and chairs too.

Have you ever seen an oak tree? There are quite a lot around here and I thought I'd like to bring one to show you. You might think I'd have to be pretty strong to bring a tree to the church and to carry it up the steps of the pulpit, but I managed it. Actually it's not a very big tree. It's not even a small tree yet, but it will be one day if it's planted, and I mean to plant it right after church.

Here it is – it's an acorn. There's an old poem which says:

"Large streams from little fountains flow,
Tall oaks from little acorns grow."

And that's true.

Once you were a little baby. Now you are a big girl or boy. One day you'll be fine women and men.

So it is with other things, things like bad habits, a little lie, a little cruelty, a little dishonesty can grow and grow until your whole life, and lots of other lives, are spoiled. And so it is with good habits, a little kindness, a little cheerfulness, a little prayer, if it is said sincerely, can have all sorts of wonderful results.

———————— · ————————

MONEY, TOKENS AND STAMPS

Children for sale

The other day, girls and boys, I was in a railway station, and I saw a strange poster on a notice board.

It read, "Children for only twenty-five pence each."

Now, there's a bargain, I thought. You couldn't expect to buy even the smallest baby for twenty-five pence. We're a little short of girls in the Manse, so, making sure I had fifty pence in my pocket, I decided that I'd have two. I thought that one with red hair and one with fair hair would be nice.

Mind you, it seemed a bit odd that anyone should be putting children up for sale, particularly British Rail, and particularly at a bargain price.

Sure enough, when I asked the man at the booking office, he said they had no children in stock – only children's tickets at twenty-five pence each.

It was very sad, but I should have known. No father or mother would sell a child – not for twenty-five pence, nor for twenty-five million pence, nor even for all the pence in the world.

God himself has put a value on each of us more than all the gold and silver and precious stones the world contains. In a way it is not too easy to understand. God gave himself for each of us when he gave Jesus to be our saviour and our friend.

"Don't be afraid," Jesus said once. "You are more valuable than many sparrows;" and more valuable than all the pence the world contains. *(Matthew 10.31)*

———————— · ————————

Millionaires

Can you see what this is? It is a pound coin.

You know what a millionaire is, don't you? Somebody who has a million of these things. Well, not many of us are millionaires and we're never likely to be millionaires in pound coins. But, you know, we have millions of other things far more important than pound coins. We've all got millions of blood cells which keep us healthy and active. In our eyes we have millions of little cells – called rods and cones – which help us to see, and they're far more important than pound coins.

Every year we are each given thirty million seconds to live, and each second can be such fun.

And after life here is ended, we have for ever, millions upon millions of years, spent in the presence of God.

We're millionaires, boys and girls, millionaires with far more important things than pound coins.

Don't envy the people who have millions of pounds. We have God as our Father and his gift to us is eternal life. "The gift of God is eternal life." *(Romans 6.23)*

———————— · ————————

The communion token

I wonder if you can see what I am holding? It looks like a little square coin. It is made out of soft lead and on it are written some letters and a date, 1699. It is a communion token. In the old days, when members of the Church came for communion services, they each handed in one of these little tokens. It is amazing that this little square of lead should have lasted all these years. There are not many things in our town as old as that; only one or two buildings. Most of the furniture, the pots and pans, the carts and carriages, the clocks and ornaments, have disappeared, as if they had never been. The further you go back in history, the less things there are which have survived.

Very little remains, from Jesus' time, almost two thousand years ago. All the treasures in Herod's palace have disappeared. All the weapons which Pilate's soldiers used, the thirty pieces of silver Judas was given, the Great Temple of Jerusalem itself – all gone. Things like these, money, buildings, weapons, *seem* to be very lasting, but they're not. That is why we should not think too much of things which can be stolen, or grow rusty, or decay. The things which really last are things which cannot be bought or sold, or weighed or measured, like love and truth and goodness.

One thing which has survived for two thousand years is the story of Jesus – of his life, his teachings and his love. These things shall never die, for he himself has promised, "I will be with you always, to the end of the age." *(Matthew 28.20)*

——————— · ———————

Blotting out the view

Do you see what I have, boys and girls? Two pennies. That's not much nowadays, although when I was a boy, I used to be given a "Saturday penny" for pocket money, just one penny. Look in your pockets and see if you're as rich as I am. If you are, bring out your two pennies. If you haven't two pennies, five-pence pieces will do.

Pennies aren't very big. To the people at the back of the church, this penny will seem just a tiny dot which they can hardly see. Hold one penny in each hand, between your thumb and your first finger. Now bring them nearer and nearer to your eyes. They look bigger now. If you bring them close to your eyes, you'll see nothing at all. The sunshine will be blocked out, and so will the church and all the people round about.

It is a pretty silly thing to hold pennies close to your eyes, but, you know, that is just what some people do all the time. They become so interested in money, and in the things that money can buy, that they see nothing else. They hardly notice the sunshine, or the beautiful things in the world, or even other people.

I think that is what Jesus was warning us about when he said, "I tell you not to be worried about the food and drink you need in order to stay alive, or about clothes for your body." *(Matthew 6.25)*

Stamps

Do you know what a Penny Black is? Of course you do. It was the first ever postage stamp, issued in 1840. Now it's worth hundreds of pounds. Actually, there is one stamp which is worth many thousands of pounds – a one cent Guinea stamp. I have one here, or at least a picture of one!

But I have a much more valuable stamp, and it is not a picture – it is a real one. It is a 1984 British 13p stamp. It is the most valuable stamp in the world if you want to post a letter. An ordinary stamp is far more useful than an old, rare one.

If you put a Penny Black on a letter, the Post Office would be very cross. They want you to use a 13p brown stamp.

What is true of stamps is true of people. Sometimes we wish we were great or rich or famous. We shouldn't. God has some things for us to do which even the richest, cleverest person in the world couldn't do. Don't think of yourself or of anybody else as common. God has made each of us and we are all his children. He loves us, every one of us, and there is something for every one of us to do for him that nobody else could do.

TRACES LEFT BEHIND

st J.

The broken mirror

During the last war a ship was torpedoed in the Indian Ocean. Most of the crew got away in a lifeboat. Day after day they drifted, getting hungrier and thirstier and more exhausted all the time. Then one day they saw, high in the sky, an aeroplane. They knew that they would never be seen by the pilot unless they had some way of attracting his attention, and they had no rockets or smoke signals, not even a lamp. Suddenly, one of the sailors remembered that he had a broken piece of mirror. Not much use, you might say, but he took it out, and caught the rays of the sun in it, and kept on flashing. The pilot of the plane noticed them and very soon help was on its way. Even though they had no light of their own, they were able to use the strong light of the sun to be saved.

In a way that is why we come to church to worship God and to say our prayers. It is not that we have much goodness ourselves, but we can reflect into the world some of the light which comes from God. "We all reflect as in a mirror the splendour of the Lord." *(2 Corinthians 3.18)*

---· ---

Fingerprints

Last week a horrid thing happened to a friend of mine who is a goldsmith – burglars broke into his workshop and stole all sorts of precious things. They left a dreadful mess behind them, broken glass, spent matches and so on. After a while the police came. They didn't tidy up the mess. Indeed they did a very strange thing

121

which made the mess even worse. They spread a white powder over everything and then they looked very carefully at the area where they had spread the powder and took lots of photographs. What were they looking for? They were looking for something which the burglars had left behind. As well as the broken glass and the spent matches there was something which they did not know they had left behind. What was it? Fingerprints.

Of course, we all leave fingerprints on everything we touch – on door handles and furniture, on knives and forks and spoons, on books and on towels. But we leave signs of ourselves in other ways too. We leave signs on other people's lives. Everybody we meet is happier or less happy after they have met us, braver or less brave, better or worse. It would be wonderful if everybody we met was a little better for having met us.

There's only one way of making sure that will be so, and that is if we learn about Jesus and try to be like him. For we ourselves are always better, kinder, and braver for having thought about him and for having been with him.

——————— · ———————

A new suit

Boys and girls, do you think I need a new suit? Everybody in the Manse seems to think I do, although it's not much more than four years since I bought the last one. So on Monday I went all the way to Glasgow to see if I could buy one in the Sales. Well, the first shop I went to had a suit made of the cloth I like, dark blue with a thin white stripe, and it was the right price too. So I tried it on. But I think it must have been made for a scarecrow like Wurzel Gummidge, and nobody could call me a scarecrow! So we moved on to shop number two. There was a nice suit there and I tried it on, but it must have been made for someone like Billy Bunter – enormously fat with little short legs – and I'm not fat, at least not enormously fat! In the third shop there was a suit the right length and the right width – but oh, girls and boys – the colour! It was a kind of yellowy-green shade. You could have seen me coming a mile off. The assistant there said to me sadly "I think you'd better get a suit to order." I haven't done it yet, but I suppose I shall.

Actually, the only way of making sure you get a suit to fit is to have it made to measure, because no two people are exactly alike. Even twins are never exactly the same. Their mothers and fathers can tell which is which.

God has made each of us different from the other four thousand million people in the world. Even our fingerprints are different from every other person's, according to the police.

It is a bit of a nuisance and a bit of expense to have to get a suit of clothes made to order, but I'm rather glad that God has made nobody else exactly and precisely like me!

God has called each of us by our own name and this year, and in all years to come, he has his separate and distinct plans for every one of us. And when our lives on earth are ended, he has prepared a place for each of us in Heaven.

The vital clue

It's not only very wrong to steal, boys and girls, it is very silly too, for sooner or later you'll be caught. I read in a newspaper recently about a thief who was even sillier than most. He had been stealing from a shop but when he ran away he left his pocket-book behind. In the pocket-book was a photograph of himself. The police found the pocket-book, looked at the photo and recognised the man. Off they went and arrested him, and soon after he was sent to prison for two whole months. You can imagine that he is pretty angry with himself for leaving his picture at the scene of the crime.

But you know, we all leave pictures of ourselves wherever we go. We leave behind us a picture of the sort of people we are – tidy or untidy, happy or miserable, good-tempered or bad, kind or unkind.

There's one way of making sure that the picture you leave behind you is always good and happy, and that is to spend as much time as you can in learning about Jesus, and thinking about him. It would be wonderful if the picture we left of ourselves was of someone like Jesus, so that people would know we were his friends. "They realized then that they had been companions of Jesus." *(Acts 4.13)*

Confetti

Last night I walked over to the church with a friend, a minister. As we came into the churchyard he said "I see you had a wedding today." Well, that was true, and a very nice wedding it was too, but my friend was not there. I wonder how he knew? He hadn't come to Dunblane till after the wedding. He hadn't heard about it. He hadn't seen the bride, and yet he knew. I wonder how? It was something he saw on the front path which gave him the clue. What was it? Confetti. People don't throw confetti except at weddings, and so as soon as my friend saw the confetti he knew there had been a wedding. When he saw that the confetti was quite fresh and hadn't been rained on or blown away, he knew the wedding must have been quite recent. Perhaps he should have been a detective instead of a minister.

Now there are some silly people who say that there is no God just because they haven't seen him. It is true our God is an invisible God, but he has given us all sorts of signs of his presence – the flowers, the trees, the stars, the smile on the face of a friend, the love that was waiting for you when you were born and which has watched over you ever since. These are the signs of God, as sure proof that he's been near as the confetti of the wedding. Although we have never seen him, we know by these signs that he is not far away from any one of us. In Jesus he has come closest of all, for we can see shining through the life of Jesus Christ the glory of the invisible God.

51.

The pawprint

Have you ever been to Canterbury in the south of England? One thing you must see if you go there is a piece of pavement which was made in the days of the Romans, seventeen hundred years ago or more. If you do see the Roman pavement, look out for a particular piece of tile on which you can see quite clearly the pawprint of a dog. When the tile was made it must have been put out into the sun to dry and a careless dog must have walked across it, leaving a mark which has lasted nearly two thousand years.

We all leave traces of one kind or another behind us. As we go through life we leave either a trail of hurt and unhappiness, or else a trail of joy and smiles, and these traces last, not for two hundred or two thousand years, but for ever, for God remembers always the good we have tried to do. Jesus will say at the last, "Come you that are blessed by my Father for I was hungry and you fed me, thirsty and you gave me a drink; I was a stranger and you received me in your homes, naked and you clothed me; I was sick and you took care of me, in prison and you visited me." *(Matthew 25.35)*

The visiting card

The other day I called to see a lady in the congregation but she was not at home. The next day I met her in the High Street and she said, "I'm very sorry I was not at home when you called."

Now I had not told anyone I'd been to this particular house. No one saw me coming in or going away from it. The question I want to ask you is, "How did the lady know I had visited her house?"

Well, I'll show you the answer. It is a tiny square of cardboard. It is a visiting card and it has my name on it. If people are not in when I call I sometimes leave one of these cards so that they will know that I'm sorry I did not see them and that some other day I'll hope to have a chat with them.

God is like that. In the Bible we are told twice that he visited the world. In Psalm 65 we read, "You visit the earth and water it," and though we don't see him he leaves a visiting card – I'll show you one now. It is a snowdrop, proof that God is once again visiting the earth, making the grass and flowers and trees grow and causing everything to come to life.

And there is another place in the Bible, in the Gospel of Luke, where we are told that the Lord God visited and redeemed his people. That is when he came in Jesus Christ, and the visiting card he left behind for all of us who did not see him was that record of what Jesus said and did which we call the Gospels. Indeed the whole Bible is the visiting card of God, the proof that he is not far from any of us and that one day he will meet and speak with us all and have us to stay with him for ever.

———————— · ————————

Fair Isle pattern

I've brought something to show you, girls and boys. It does not belong to me and I had to borrow it specially for the occasion. It is a jersey, a very beautiful jersey. But it's not the jersey I want you to look at. It is the design knitted into it. I wonder if you know what it is called? It is a Fair Isle pattern and it is called that because the only place where it is knitted is in Fair Isle, an island between Orkney and Shetland. The people in Fair Isle have been knitting this pattern ever since 1588. In that year a great fleet of sailing ships set off from Spain to attack England. But this fleet, the Armada, did not do very well. A great storm sprang up and the ships were blown everywhere and a great number were wrecked. One was wrecked on Fair Isle. The people of Fair Isle were very kind to the shipwrecked Spanish sailors and many of them settled down to live there. In return for the kindness they received they taught the people in Fair Isle how to knit this pattern which is now so well known. Though they lived and died so long ago, the Spanish sailors left a pattern which the people of Fair Isle have copied ever since.

Long before the Armada, the Lord Jesus Christ came to earth. People were not in the least kind to him and finally killed him, but before he died he gave them a pattern, an example of how to live.

Now all over the world there are people who are trying to copy the example of Jesus, to live their lives with some of the kindness and courage he showed.

He's ready to teach us too, if we let him. "Learn from me," he once said, and there is no better, finer Master from whom to learn.

Traces in the snow

I like to get up early in the morning and so I usually bring in the milk. The trouble is that I can never tell if the milkman has been or not, and I don't like to put my nose out of the door these cold mornings unless the milk is there waiting to be taken in.

But one or two mornings this week I looked out of the Manse window and something there told me that the milkman had been. You know how I knew, don't you? I saw his footprints in the snow from the gate all the way up the path.

Of course it is not only the milkman who leaves signs behind him showing where he has been. If you go into the bathroom after some boys you will see paw marks on the towels, the soap in the water and water on the floor. Of if you go into a room where some girls have been you will will find shoes and books, and toys and dolls all over the place.

Indeed all of us, grown-ups too, leave signs behind us showing where we've been. If we are selfish and bad-tempered we leave people miserable and unhappy. If we are cheerful and kind, we leave them smiling and happy.

Wherever Jesus went, he left people happier, better and healthier than he had found them, and so will we if we try to be like him.

———————— · ————————

CLOCKS, COMPASSES AND OTHER USEFUL THINGS

The King's clock

I wonder how many of you have a wrist watch of your own? If you look at it, you will probably find that it has twelve numbers on it, written 1, 2, 3, 4, 5 and so on (unless it is a digital watch). But some watches have numbers written differently – in roman numerals. The church clock is like that, and so is Big Ben, which you see on television sometimes. In roman numerals you write I for 1, then two ones for two, three ones for three; but what is it for four? IV. Yes, that is usually true, but not on clocks and watches. Always on a clock, four is shown as four single ones, IIII.

This all began six hundred years ago. King Charles of France ordered a clock from a clockmaker called Henry. When the clock was ready, Henry showed it to to the King, who happened to be in a bad temper that day. The King pointed to the IV, with which Henry had marked four o'clock. "That is wrong," said the King. "It should be IIII, four ones." "No," said Henry, "IV is correct." But the King did not like to be argued with, so he ordered poor Henry to take the clock away and change IV to IIII. Henry just had to do as he was told, and every clockmaker and every watchmaker since has copied the mistake poor Henry was forced to make.

It just shows how important it is to set a good example. All the time, your little brothers and sisters and the boy or girl next door may be watching you and possibly trying to imitate you. Whenever you do or say anything wrong, they may well do or say the same. Someone else seeing or hearing them will copy them, and so your lie or your wrong-doing will go on growing, leading other people astray whom you have never even seen.

Now, every time you see those four ones on a clock, make up your mind not to be like cross old King Charles, who not only went wrong himself, but led so many others astray.

There's only one way of making sure that we neither go wrong ourselves nor lead others astray, and that is to follow Jesus as closely as we can. Jesus said, "I have set an example for you, so that you will do just what I have done for you." (John 13.15)

A luminous face

We have a clock in our house, a perfectly ordinary clock. At least it looks perfectly ordinary in the daytime, but at night when it's dark the hands and the figures of the clock glow. The darker it becomes, the more clearly they shine. It has what is called a luminous face.

You probably have a clock like that in your house too. If so, there is something you can learn from it, and that is to be brightest when all around is dark. When things go wrong and people are miserable, then we should be all the more encouraging and cheerful. The darker things become, the more we should try to be helpful and kind.

We will only learn to be like that if we take as our model Jesus, our Lord, who said of himself, "I am come a light into the world, that whosoever believeth on me should not abide in darkness." (John 12.46)

The Salisbury clock

Have you ever been to Salisbury Cathedral? It's famous for two things. It has the tallest spire in England and it has the oldest clock in England, possibly in the world. The clock was made in 1386, over 600 years ago. It wasn't working for seventy-two years, but even so, it has ticked its way through more than five hundred years.

Do you know how many ticks there are in five hundred years, boys and girls? Over fifteen billion, and that's a lot of ticks. Fifteen billion. Do you know how the old clock kept going for fifteen billion ticks? Well, I'll tell you – one tick at a time.

That's the secret of doing anything worthwhile in life. Don't worry about yesterday, nor about tomorrow. Just live each day as well as you can. Jesus once said, "Don't worry about tomorrow." If we trust God's love for us, we shall face each week, each day, each hour unafraid.

We shall live like the old clock – one tick at a time.

The clock which tells lies

A lie is a horrible thing, boys and girls. No matter how much you may be tempted to, don't tell lies.

You would think there would be no lies in the Manse. Well, I'm sorry to tell you that there is a lie told in the Manse every half-hour, day and night. It is not Mrs. Gray who tells lies, and it is not I. It is a clock, an old chiming clock. It is supposed to chime out hours from one to twelve, and to strike once every half-hour. But instead it strikes once every hour and at each half-hour it strikes any number it likes. Sometimes in the early afternoon, when somebody has come to see me, it suddenly strikes twelve and they think they have stayed much too long.

The trouble with the bad old clock is that its voice and its hands never agree.

We're sometimes just as bad. Our voices say one thing, but our hands do something different. We say that we'll help to clear the table or to wash the dishes, but we start looking at television and our hands don't do what our voices have said.

We say we're Christians, but our hands don't do the sort of things Christ did and which he wants us to do. He said, "You are my friends," not if you say you are but "if you do what I command you." *(John 15.14)*

Seven days plus one

In the Manse we have a grandfather clock. It keeps splendid time, although it is nearly two hundred years old. I wind it every Saturday night, just as my father and my grandfather used to do. After it is wound, it keeps going for a week.

One Saturday I forgot all about it. Do you know what happened? Nothing! It just kept on going. The old clockmakers knew that people could sometimes forget to do the things they ought to do, so they made their clocks to go after they were wound, not just for a week, but for a week and a day.

Perhaps you and I could learn from the old clock, learn to do just a little bit more than we are forced to do, to give a little bit more than we must give, and in helpfulness to go just a little bit further than we have to go. If your mother asks you to bring a bucketful of coal, bring two. If she asks you to set tea, wash up afterwards also. If everybody in the country and the world were to go the extra mile, were to do the extra piece of work, were just a little more helpful and kind, it would be a very different country and a very different world.

Jesus said, "If a man makes you go one mile, go with him two." *(Matthew 5.41) (N.E.B.)*

The clock which went backwards

Do you have an electric clock in your house? Clocks are grand things – so long as they go. Our clock stopped the other day but someone must have started it again. The next morning I looked at it and it said "eight o'clock." I wrote a few letters and looked again. Now, to my astonishment, it said "half-past seven." I thought I must have misread it the first time, and was glad to have so much time to spare. In a few minutes I looked again. It said "twenty-five minutes past seven." Something was clearly wrong.

Whoever had started it the day before had started it going backwards! If I'd left it, it would soon have been yesterday and, later on, the day before. Quite soon it would have been last year! That would be a fine kind of clock to have in the morning when you are late for school, or when an examination was very near. It would be fun, too, to have a clock going backwards on 26th December, or the day after a birthday, or on the last day of the holidays. Alas, although you can make the clock go backwards, you cannot turn time backwards. Yesterday is past and gone for ever. You cannot have it again. You cannot undo the things you did yesterday or unsay the things you said. That is why we should always pray that we may keep our hands from evil and our lips from lies, for "yesterday . . . is past." *(Psalm 90.4)*

———————— · ————————

The five minute clock

I was given a very special kind of clock the other day, boys and girls. It's a very small clock and it doesn't go for very long. You know how electric clocks go on for ever, and some clocks go for eight days, and most for at least twenty-four hours? Well, mine just goes for five minutes. It doesn't need electricity and it doesn't need winding up. Although it only goes for five minutes, it is all the more useful if you're boiling an egg and don't want a hard one.

You would like to see my little clock? It's a sand-glass – an egg-timer. Two little bulbs of glass joined in the middle.

It starts off with all the sand in the top half and the sand trickles through, a grain at a time. In exactly five minutes all the sand is in the bottom half, and if you want another five minutes' worth, you must turn it upside down.

The sand-glass has its own little sermon to preach. Just as the little pile of sand is made up of lots of little grains, so time is made up of lots of little seconds. After all, a minute is made up of only sixty seconds and an hour of only sixty minutes, twelve turns of my little sand-glass. A day is only twenty-four separate hours and a year only three hundred and sixty-five days, or three hundred and sixty-six in a leap year.

Do you know the little poem which goes:

Little drops of water,
Little grains of sand,
Make the mighty ocean
And the pleasant land.?

Life itself is made up of lots of little things – little joys, little duties, little deeds of kindness, little words of cheer.

Don't waste your time dreaming of the wonderful things you're going to do one day, or the great things you could do if you lived somewhere else.

Start now, and fill today and tomorrow with little bits of kindness and usefulness and cheer, and you will not have lived in vain.

As the old prophet Zechariah once said, "Who has despised the day of small things?" *(Zechariah 4.10)*

How to shorten sermons

Are my sermons too long? Don't tell me. One family in the congregation says that they are. Not the father of the family, he's a decent man. But the mother and the boys are always saying, "We didn't get out till twenty, or twenty-five past twelve."

Well, I've decided to stop that entirely. So I've bought a very special watch. It's meant for ministers, because it is called a "stop-watch". Now, when it reaches twelve o'clock, if you press this little button, it will stop. Unfortunately, I won't!

Whether a watch or a clock is stopped or not, time goes on; whether we sleep or wake, work or play, time still goes on.

There are only sixty seconds in one minute, sixty minutes in one hour; only twenty-four hours in one day and seven days in one week; fifty-two weeks in one year and only so many years in one life. That is why we shouldn't waste time in silly things or wicked things.

The Psalmist prayed, and we should pray too, "Teach us to number our days." *(Psalm 90.12)*

Jesus the compass

Do you know what a compass is, boys and girls? It shows us the direction of north, and so we can work out where south, east and west are. Compasses are used by mountaineers and desert travellers, but mostly by sailors, for there are no roads marked on the sea and no direction posts to tell one where to go. But a friend of mine in America has a compass in his car, and this is why. One day he was in Minnesota, in the very middle of the United States, where the roads are flat and straight and where there are very few towns and villages. He was driving along and found he was short of petrol, so he turned into a filling station. He spent a little time there, he got his petrol and had his tyres checked and so on. Finally, all was ready and he drove off. He had driven many miles before he came to a town that looked very familiar. Where do you think he was? He was right back where he had started from. When he had come out of the filling station, instead of turning left he had turned right and had driven all the way back down the road he had come. No wonder he always carries a compass now.

There is not much use driving far or driving fast if you are driving in the wrong direction, and that is true of life too. That is why we should obey the command which Christ gave to people long ago and which he gives to us now. It is "follow me." For if we do, he will never let us go astray, but will lead us in the right direction from the beginning of our lives right to the end.

Jesus is our measuring tape

I'm holding something in my hand this morning which is exactly six feet long. Can you guess what it is? It is made of steel, half an inch broad and quite thin. It is a steel tape-measure and it is a very handy thing. There's probably one in your own house. Your parents will use it often. If you're putting up curtains, or making a dress, or building a shed, you've got to make accurate measurements, and the only way to do that is to use something which we know to be correct, like a tape-measure.

That is what we are doing every Sunday in church and Sunday School. We take the only perfect life that has ever been lived, the life of our Lord Jesus Christ, and we measure our lives against it and see where we've gone wrong and ask his help to put things right.

Jesus once said, "I have given you an example, so that you may do as I have done." (John 13.15)

The fault-finding chart

Did you get a diary for Christmas? I did. It has all sorts of information in it – high tide at London Bridge; quarter-days in Ireland; weights and measures. There are all sorts of special diaries you can get, for Guides, Scouts, B.B., and so on. One year I got a Motorists' Diary. It had maps in it, lighting-up times, road signs, registration numbers. There was one thing in it I didn't find very useful. It was called a fault-finding chart. I don't need that at all. I can find lots of faults in my car. It's got bits of rust here and there, and makes some strange noises, and has things which don't work as they should. I know its faults without any chart. What I do not know is how to correct them and put things right.

That's not so easy.

You know, it might not be a bad idea to have a fault-finding chart in every diary, not about faults in cars, but about faults in people.

(1) Did you tell any lies today?

(2) Did you steal today?

(3) Did you lose your temper today?

(4) Were you mean to someone today?

That would be a good kind of fault-finding chart.

For, though it is easy to see where other people go wrong and to see faults in them, it is not so easy sometimes to see faults in ourselves.

The best way is to learn more and more about Jesus, how good and true and kind he was, and to check our faults against his faultlessness. Then we must ask him to cleanse us from our faults and to help us each day, each week, each year, to grow more like him.

God's early-warning system

When I was in a church the other day, a bell suddenly started ringing. It was not the pleasant, sonorous sort of bell one hears from a church tower. It was a noisy, disagreeable, electric bell. It was, in fact, a fire-alarm. Fortunately, it was a false alarm on this occasion, for no fire was to be found. It seemed a pity that in a lovely church there should have to be such a nasty, loud bell. But fire is a terrible thing. If it does break out, it is best to know about it at once, so that it can be put out right away.

There are other things which are just as destructive and terrible as fire – things like lies and cruelty and dishonesty. When any of these break out in our lives, God's alarm system sounds loud and clear, ringing a bell deep within us. What do we call God's warning system? Yes, it is conscience.

Of course, we do not need to pay any attention to our consciences. We can just go on doing the sort of things we know we should not do. But if we do, if we ignore God's alarm bell, we run the risk of the bad things spreading, till our lives are spoiled and perhaps the lives of other people round about us as well.

So, as Jiminy Cricket used to say, we should always let our conscience be our guide, or, as St. Paul wrote to the Hebrews, "Have a good conscience in all things." *(Hebrews 13.18)*

Reflections

In my hand I've something rather wonderful. If I look at it, I see one thing. If you look at it, you see something different. If your mother looks at it, she sees something different still. And yet it is the same thing. It looks different to everyone in the whole world. What is it?

If I tell you that what I see is a plain-looking, middle-aged man.

If you look at it, you'll see a pretty young girl or a good-looking boy. If your mother looks at it, she'll see a nice lady. What is it? It's a mirror, of course.

A marvellous thing, a mirror. It gives a different picture to everybody who looks at it. A more marvellous thing would be a mirror which showed us ourselves, not as we are, but as we would like to be, perhaps with rosy cheeks, or long, wavy hair.

But you know, boys and girls, we have a mirror which shows us ourselves, not as we are, not as we would like to be, but as we should be and as at last, with God's help, we shall be.

In the life of Jesus, we see what our lives were meant to be like and what they shall be like if we ask God to help, and if we make Jesus the example, the pattern, and the model of our lives.

For God has promised that finally we shall be like him.

———————— · ————————

The old lady and gentleman

I've brought my house for you to see this morning, girls and boys. It's not the Manse. It's a very special kind of house.

In this house there are no children, just an old gentleman and his wife. They are a very clever old couple, for they always know what the weather is going to be like. If it is going to be wet, the old gentleman comes out. If it is going to be fine and dry, the old lady comes out. But the sad thing is that they never come out together, which seems a pity.

There are some people in the church who are like the old gentleman. They never come out to the church when it is fine. They don't bother with God when everything is going well.

There are some people in the church who are like the old lady. They never come out to church when it is wet, but only when it is fine. If things go badly for them, they forget all about God.

Some are "Wet Weather Christians."

Some are "Fair Weather Christians."

But the only Christians that are any use at all are the "All Weather Christians."

That is why Christ's friends in the Book of Acts said, "We will give ourselves full time to praying and working." *(Acts 6.4)*

---·---

Field glasses

I like to see who is in church and who is not. In this big church I found that I could see the people at the front, and the people halfway back, and the people three quarters way back. But try as I might I couldn't see those at the very back.

I was thinking about it and suddenly I got a good idea. All I need is a pair of field glasses and I can see everybody, the boy who eats sweeties during the lesson, the man who sleeps during the sermon and the girl who fidgets. You've no idea what fun it is. I wish I could do this every Sunday – but perhaps I had better not. Lots of visitors come to the church and they might think I was a bit odd.

Anyway, perhaps it does not matter whether I see you in church or not. God sees you and that is all that matters. Wherever we are by day or night, whatever we are doing, God is looking at us with wise and kind and understanding eyes, eyes like the eyes of Christ – glad when we do well, but always looking at us with love.

Perhaps we'd do better, be kinder, truer and more faithful if we remembered some words from the Old Testament, "The Lord looks down from heaven." *(Psalm 14.2)*

---·---

Braille

What do you read with, boys and girls? That's an easy one to answer. You read with your eyes, don't you? But not everybody does. Those who are unfortunate enough to be blind read with their fingers. Their books and magazines are not covered with print like ours. They are sheets covered with little raised dots. This kind of printing for the blind is called "Braille" after the clever man who invented it. (You can see these sheets of Braille after the service, if you like.)

God spoke to people by the words of the prophets, but people were deaf and wouldn't listen. God spoke to people by the beauty of this wonderful world, but people were blind and couldn't see. So God at last spoke to people in a different way – by his son, Jesus Christ.

God has said all he had to say in the birth and life and death of Jesus Christ, his son, our Lord. As we learn more about Jesus, so we learn more about God. Just as blind folk read Braille, so we may read what God has to say in Jesus Christ.

St. Paul tells us, "God has spoken to us through his son." (*Hebrews 1.2*)

———————— · ————————

Meters

One day last week a man came to our door. Quite possibly he came to yours too. He came in. He didn't come into the study to see me. He didn't go into the sitting-room or even into the kitchen. Of all places, he went into the cupboard in the hall. He had a small torch with him and a book and a pencil. He wrote something in the book, and then he went away. Who was he? He was the man from the electricity board and he was reading our meter. He was the meter man. You know what a meter is, don't you?

Then a terrible thing happened. Another man came and he carried a meter with him, and do you know where he put it? In my little boy's mouth! Actually, it was the doctor who put it in and it was a very special type of meter. I'll show you one. It is a thermo-meter, a meter to measure heat or temperature.

There are other kinds of meter too – an alti-meter to measure height, a speedo-meter to measure how fast the car is going, and a chrono-meter which measures how fast time is going.

A meter is something utterly reliable by which we can measure things like how hot we are, how fast we're going, or how high up we are.

I wonder if you know if there is a way of measuring how good we are? Of course, there is. That is what God has given us Christ for, so that, looking at his life, we may know how we are meant to be – good and kind and gentle and loving and pure.

Jesus himself once said, "I have given you an example." (*John* 13.15)

———————— · ————————

The dictionary

Are you sometimes given book tokens as presents, boys and girls? What kind of book do you buy – adventure stories, school stories, fairy stories, space stories?

One of the most useful books you could buy would be one like this. It's a marvellous book. It's not the Bible, but every word that is in the Bible is here. Every word you've ever read or written is here. Every word that Scott or Dickens ever wrote, every word of my sermon, every word in the English language is here.

What is it?

A dictionary.

If you don't have a good dictionary, you should buy one. It is a very useful thing.

Mark you, once you have a dictionary, don't think that right away you'll be able to write books with it. All the words are here, but you've still got to get them in the right order. It's no use just taking a word here and a word there and hoping it will make sense. It won't. It is no use having the right words unless you get them in the right order.

That is true of life as well. It is full of interesting things – work and play, books and hobbies, holidays, friendships, religion. But the art of living is to get them in the correct order.

Jesus, who lived a finer life than anyone else has ever lived, said that the secret of life was to put God first in our lives and then everything else would fall into its proper place.

That is what he meant when he said, "Be concerned above everything else with the Kingdom of God and with what he requires of you, and he will provide you with all these other things." *(Matthew 6.33)*

CHRISTIAN LIFE

FORGIVENESS

s.t. ✓

Horrible Corner

There once was a great painter called Burne-Jones. When he was old, he lived with his daughter and with her daughter, that is, his granddaughter. I don't know her name. Let's call her Mary.

Mostly Mary was good. Sometimes she was not so good. Sometimes she was bad. When she was bad, her mother used to make her go and stand in the darkest, dreariest corner of the room, where there was nothing to see but blank walls. Mary thought of it as Horrible Corner. One evening she was as bad as bad could be. She wouldn't do a thing she was told, was cheeky to her mother and began to sulk when she was spoken to about it. So finally her mother made her go and stand in Horrible Corner till it was time to go to bed.

When she got up in the morning, she was still feeling miserable, as one does if one has been bad. When she went downstairs, her grandfather was waiting for her and he was smiling. He asked her to look at Horrible Corner. When she looked, she began to smile too, for the walls were no longer blank and empty. Her grandfather had been up early and all over the walls he had painted rabbits and spring lambs and ducklings and flowers. He had turned Horrible Corner into Happy Corner.

That is what Jesus does when he forgives us. He takes away all our bad tempers and miseries and gives us good and happy thoughts instead. Then he says to us, what once he said to someone who had been very bad indeed, "I do not condemn you . . . Go, but do not sin again." *(John 8.11)*

—————— · ——————

Master Nobody

Have you ever been told that you are the worst boy in the world? Quite often, I expect, if you *are* a boy, that is. Well, it's not true! For I know the worst boy in the world and he is not any of you. Sometimes you are as good as gold – but the worst boy in the world is never good. From morning to night, from Sunday to Saturday, year in, year out, he is busy, busy being bad. Would you like to know his name? It is a very funny name. It is Master Nobody. He is always up to mischief. When a cake disappears before the visitors come, and Mother asks, "Who ate it?", the answer is, "Nobody." It is "Nobody" who spills the ink on the carpet. "Nobody" teases the dog. "Nobody" makes all the noise in the house. "Nobody" breaks ornaments. "Nobody" takes the apples that seem to melt from the trees. He leaves the gates and doors open behind him. He is a terrible fellow, is "Master Nobody" – a nasty, untidy, unthoughtful boy. There is not a wicked thing that he is not blamed for. So much so, that I wonder if he is not sometimes blamed for things he never did at all. He has such a bad name that Willie and John, and sometimes even Jean and Mary, blame him for doing things they have done themselves.

We all do the wrong thing at times, boys and girls, and grown-ups too – often without really meaning to. The pity of it is that when we are found out, instead of being frank about it and owning up, we become cross and tell lies, accusing "Nobody," or anybody but ourselves. But God cannot forgive us and help us to do and to be better until we are ready to admit where we have gone wrong. That is what St. Paul meant when he said, "If we say that we have no sin, we deceive ourselves, and the truth is not in us. If we confess our sins, God is faithful and just to forgive us our sins, and to cleanse us from all unrighteousness." *(1 John 1.8, 9)*

What's in my pocket?

I have something in my pocket, boys and girls, and I want you to guess what it is. It has length and breadth, but no thickness. It has no weight and no colour, but it has a shape. If I were to tell one of your mothers about it, she would want to take it away. Mrs. Gray *will* take it away tomorrow, but when she has taken it away, it will not exist any more. I suspect that some of you have one too, at this very moment. If I tell you where you might have it, you would probably guess what it is. You might have one in the heel of your sock or in the finger of your glove. Yes! It is a hole. That is not much to boast about, is it?

There are a great many things we have which, like the hole, are not worth having, which we would be far better without. There are, for example, bad habits like telling lies or swearing, and bad tempers and gloomy moods. We would all be far better without these. It was to help us to get rid of these very things that Christ came into the world. The next time you watch your mother mending a hole, think of Jesus who came "to take away our sins." *(1 John 3.5)*

PUTTING GOD FIRST

A scissor

Girls and boys, what is this? It's a scissor. What use is it? None at all. One scissor is no more use than one trouser or one tong. You've got to have a pair of scissors, a pair of trousers or a pair of tongs, before they are of any value. One without the other is worthless.

That is true of people too. We need each other. Children need parents and parents need children. Teachers need pupils or they can't be teachers, and pupils need teachers. The butcher needs the baker, and both need the doctor sometimes.

All of us in the church, the young and the old, the rich and the poor, the clever and the not quite so clever, the choir, the organist, the ministers, we all need each other. If we all stayed at home and tried to be Christians on our own, we'd be as much use as one scissor, one trouser or one tong.

There's something else. Even a pair of scissors isn't any use unless there's someone to pick them up and use them. And no matter how many people there are in church and no matter how well we work together, we're of no use at all unless we ask God to take us into his hand to use us for his great and wonderful purposes.

Jesus once said, "Without me, ye can do nothing." Like everything else that Jesus said, that's true.

—————— · ——————

First things first

Do you like spelling, girls and boys? You may not, but it is still very important. If you don't spell a word correctly, even if you have one letter out of place, it can change its whole meaning.

If I were to tell the organist that he has a great big GROAN somewhere up beside the choir, he'd be very cross, but change the O and the G and the very unmusical GROAN becomes ORGAN.

Have you ever heard of a CAT HERALD? It sounds like a newspaper for kittens, doesn't it? But if you take the D from the last place and put it between the E and the R, you'll find that the two words together make up a word you know very well.

It is very important in spelling words to have the letters in the correct order, and it is very important in life to get everything in the right place. Football is a great game, but not if we treat it as being of first importance. Food is absolutely necessary for us, but we should not spend all our time eating or thinking about eating. Television is all right in its place, but not if we look at it in every spare minute from morning till night. We have to keep things in their correct order if we are to live useful and happy lives. Above all, we must learn to put God first. Then everything else falls into its proper place. That is what Jesus meant when he said, "Seek ye first the kingdom of God and his righteousness; and all these things shall be added unto you."

Lessons

I know you love lessons, and so I thought that instead of having a talk to the children this morning, we would have some lessons. First of all we'll have some spelling, then some geography, and finally a music lesson. To make it more interesting we'll make it a kind of quiz.

First the spelling. I'm going to spell out two words which describe two things in the church, and you're going to tell me where to find them. Ready? YRANMYH, ELBIB.

Oh well, we'll move on to geography. I'm going to spell out two place-names and you're to tell me what country they are in. ENALBNUD, ENUOD.

All right? We'll try you on music now. Listen carefully and tell me what this familiar tune is. (Organist plays a simple hymn tune backwards.)

You don't know it? Let's go back to the beginning and do it again, but with a difference. YRANMYH – HYMNARY, ELBIB – BIBLE.

Now let's have a look at the two place-names. ENOUD – DOUNE, ENALBNUD – DUNBLANE.

Now we'll ask the organist to play the tune again, but the right way round this time. You see, even if you have the correct letters or the proper notes, they are no use unless they are in the proper order, with the first letter first, the second letter second and so on. Otherwise it is all muddle and confusion.

So it is in life. Unless you put God first, other people second and yourself after that, everything will be confused and upset.

Jesus said, "Seek ye first the kingdom of God and his righteousness and everything will be given to you." *(Matthew 6.33)*

――――――― · ―――――――

The ball that will not go straight

Some girls and boys think that there is only one thing to be done with a ball and that is to kick it towards some goalposts, preferably your opponents'. When you all become older, you may take a smaller ball and pat it back and forth across a net in a game called tennis. When you are very, very old you may take an even smaller ball and hit it with a stick towards a hole, and that is golf.

Then there's another game, and for it you need the hardest, heaviest ball of all. The ball is like this, and the game is called bowls. You're not given a racquet nor a stick, and you're not allowed to kick the ball. You've got to throw it so that it lands up very near to a little white ball called a "jack". It is a very difficult thing to do.

Just to make it even harder, a bowling-green bowl is made differently from other balls. Balls are usually balanced, but a bowling-green bowl is lop-sided. It has what is called a "bias" so that, no matter how you throw it, it never, ever goes straight. It always curves to the left or to the right. That is why I think bowls is the hardest game of all.

It is also why you and I are just a little bit like a bowl. There is a bias in us so that we find it very hard to go straight. We're tempted to be selfish, and bad-tempered, and lazy, and not quite honest. Left to ourselves we are always going astray.

The only wise thing to do is to put ourselves into the hands of Christ. In his hands our lives will not miss the mark but will be truly happy and useful to God and to his world.

Making that kind of success in life is far more important than making a success at bowls or golf or tennis, or even football.

Single-minded

Have you ever noticed how much more interesting other people's books are than your own? The other day I started reading a book which belonged to someone very much younger than me, and I could not lay it down till I had finished it. It was *The Story of Dr. Dolittle* by Hugh Lofting. Dr. Dolittle was the kindest man in the world – kind, not only to people, but to animals, as we all should be. The book is all about the animals and birds Dr. Dolittle knew and loved. There was Dab-Dab, the Duck; Chi-Chi, the Monkey; Too-Too, the Owl; and Grub-Grub, the Pig. The most interesting animal of all was the Pushmi-Pullyu which, instead of having a head and a tail, had a head at both ends. This must have been a handy arrangement. It meant it could talk to itself so easily. It could eat far more at parties, too, for it had two mouths instead of one. It meant, moreover, that it could speak with its mouth full – one mouth, anyway, for it had always the other to speak with. There are all sorts of advantages in having two heads.

But there was one big disadvantage – as Dab-Dab, the Duck, pointed out – and that was that the Pushmi-Pullyu had the greatest difficulty in making its mind up, for, you see, it did not have one mind to make up, but two. That is probably why there are no Pushmi-Pullyus left, even in the darkest jungle. Perhaps there never were any, except in Never-Never Land.

But there are boys and girls, and men and women, who are very like the Pushmi-Pullyu. They are always in two minds. They can never quite decide whether to do this or to do that. They shilly-shally and hesitate and change their minds a dozen times about everything. In particular, they can never quite decide whether to obey God or not. They would like to, but it is very nice to go with the crowd instead. They know they ought to, but it is so much easier to be selfish and greedy. In fact, they try at one and the same time to please God and to please themselves. But nobody can do that. If you are going to serve God you must be *single-minded* about it. As Jesus said, "No man can serve two masters. You cannot serve God and Mammon." *(Matthew 6.24)*

So do not be a Pushmi-Pullyu. Make up your mind that you are not going to serve two masters. Trust and love and obey and follow the one Master who is worthy of being loved and obeyed and followed; Jesus Christ, our Lord.

A place for everything

Some time ago I bought a can of something in a shop. At the very moment when I was handing my money over, the Government was spending vast sums in trying to burn this same stuff up, sink it to the bottom of the sea or otherwise destroy it. You can guess what I was buying, a can of oil. The Government was trying to destroy it because, while oil is very useful in the right place, it is very bad in the wrong place, when it fouls beaches and kills lovely sea birds. This it did when the *Torrey Canyon*, the great oil tanker, sank near the Isles of Scilly.

Oil is a little like something else, something which boys have some or most of the time, and girls too, something you don't specially want but cannot give away. Your mother is always trying to take it away, but she doesn't in the least need it for herself. It is the commonest thing in the world, the most useful in some places, and a great nuisance in others. If I tell you that it is apt to get on your hands and knees, you will know what it is – dirt. Dirt is a good thing in the right place. Flowers grow in it and vegetables and grain and trees. Only when it gets into the wrong place is it bad.

There is a place for everything in life if we can only keep it there, a place for play and a place for work, a place for laughter and a place for seriousness. The secret of life is to get everything in its right place. We shall do that if we give God his right place in our lives, the first place. He will show us how to make our lives fine and good, how to "put a difference between the clean and the unclean." *(Leviticus 10.10)*

GOD'S LOVE FOR US

Through the night

What were you doing all night, girls and boys? Well, you know the answer to that one. You were sound asleep in your beds. So was I. But not everybody was. There are always some policemen on duty. There is a doctor on call should you really need one. All night long trains go up and down the lines. Long before you are awake the cows are being milked, the newspapers printed, the letters sorted, the bread and rolls baked. If you *should* be awake during the night, you can switch on the light, and that means that someone is on duty at the power-station. We should really think more often about the people who stay awake so that we may sleep without being anxious or afraid.

We should certainly take time every night to remember God, who will watch over us so that we may sleep safely and unafraid. Unlike us, God never gets tired. He doesn't need to sleep.

So every night when we fall asleep we should remember the words of Psalm 121, "He that keepeth thee will not slumber, Behold he that keepeth Israel shall neither slumber nor sleep."

——————— · ———————

The Get Better card

Boys and girls, what's this? It's not a Christmas card. It's not an Easter card. It's not a Birthday card. It's a Get Well card.

I've often thought a better name for it would be a "Get Better" card. If you're really ill you can't just get well in a day, but no matter how ill you are, you can be a little bit better every day.

It is nice to know that our friends are sorry when we're ill and that they want us to get better.

There's one friend we all have when we're ill. He not only wants us to get better, he does something about it. He gives us a very special Get Better card, one that actually helps us to be well again. Here is one. No flowers on it. No nice little poem. A lot of dull printing and some very bad writing, but it really helps us to get well. What is it? A prescription. Our friend the doctor gives us a prescription to help us get well.

You know, in a way the Bible is a sort of Get Better card. It tells us not to tell lies, nor to cheat, nor to hurt our neighbours. It tells us that we ought to get better every day. We know that, but it is not always easy. God knew that it was difficult for us, and so he did more than just send us a Get Better card. He sent his son to heal and to save us all, to help us to grow better every day. If we grow daily more like Jesus then, finally, we will be perfect as he is.

Greyfriars Bobby

In many churchyards there are tombstones which have been placed there in memory of those who have died. In Greyfriars Churchyard in Edinburgh a very unusual tombstone has been erected. It is not in memory of a person but of a dog who lived a long time ago. Who can tell me the dog's name? Greyfriars Bobby. Nobody paid much attention to Bobby and his master when they moved about Edinburgh, but the time came when Bobby's master died and was buried in Greyfriars Churchyard. That night kind people were willing to give the dog a home, but he would not leave his master's grave. Nor would he the next night, nor the next, nor any night afterwards. Days and weeks and months passed. Greyfriars Bobby stayed by his master's grave right up to the day of his own death. He was a very wonderful dog indeed.

Well, you probably knew all about Greyfriars Bobby already. But does anyone know the name of his master? You should. You know someone quite well who has the same name. Greyfriars Bobby's master was called – John Gray! I often think there should be a statue to John Gray as well as to his dog, for John Gray must have loved Bobby very much for Bobby to love him so much in return.

For we learn to love from those who love us, which is why we should love God very much, for he loves us very much indeed. He has shown his love by giving us life and so much else, and at last by giving his own son Jesus Christ to be our friend and saviour.

We love God because he first loved us.

A hint on gliding

A friend of mine who is a minister in Glasgow has just taken up a new sport, and it seems to be a very dangerous one. It is gliding – flying in a plane with no engines in it. However, he has mastered the knack of it, which seems to be to use all the up-draughts and currents of air and eddies of wind.

My friend told me a very interesting thing the other day, that, when you are gliding, you do not make for the nice clear blue sky, nor even for the pretty little white clouds. You make for the big black ugly clouds, for it is only near them that you find the strong currents of air able to lift you up and keep you going.

Gliding seems to be just a little like life. If you spend your life trying to dodge work and trouble and have an easy time, you accomplish nothing significant. If you are prepared to tackle the hard and unpleasant tasks you will find that there is a zest and an interest in them which will make life far more thrilling and worthwhile. All sorts of help comes to those who are prepared to deny themselves and turn their backs on safe and easy ways of living. Above all, God is never nearer to us than when our difficulties are greatest. "If any man will come after me," said Christ, "let him deny himself and take up his cross and follow me." That doesn't sound an easy invitation. He did not pretend that it was. "In the world you will have trouble," he said on another occasion. But he promised that those who followed him would not have to face trouble alone. "In the world you will have trouble. But courage! victory is mine; I have conquered the world." *(John 16.33) (N.E.B.)*

USE YOUR BIBLE

Bibles are for reading

Girls and boys, I am going to ask you a question and I want you to shout out "Yes" or "No", whichever you think is the right answer. Are you ready? Here goes.

Are my sermons too long?

I think the "Noes" have it!

Actually, I shouldn't preach sermons which are too long, for there is a watch on my wrist. You can't see it, but I can. The trouble is that although I can see it, I always forget to look at it, which is very bad of me. For what is the use of having a watch, if I never look at it?

All of you have a Bible, but you might as well not have one if you forget to read it. It is a lovely church we have here, but it might as well never have been built unless you and I worship in it Sunday by Sunday.

It is wonderful that God's own son, Jesus, came down from Heaven and lived on earth and taught and healed and helped and died for all of us, but Jesus might just as well never have been born unless we learn about him and try to obey him and come to love him as he loves us.

He never forgets you, and so, whatever else you forget, "Make certain that you do not forget the Lord." *(Deuteronomy 6.12)*

———————— · ————————

Don't keep it good!

Boys and girls, do any of you have new clothes today? If you have, I wonder if your mother said to you, what my mother always used to say to me, when I was given anything new, "Now, see and keep it good!" That is only right. We should not waste things which are meant for "best".

But there are some things, the more you use them, the better. It is of no use trying to keep your brain good by not using it. The more you use it, the more you think and learn, the better your brain will be.

That is true of your muscles, too. The more you use them, the more exercise you give them, the better. It is of no use trying to keep your muscles good by not using them. They'll just spoil.

I know some boys who believe in keeping soap good, but that's not wise. Soap is meant to be used and not just kept for special occasions.

Sometimes people show me Bibles they got as prizes when they were at Sunday School and say, "Look, it's just like new." They seem to feel they should be congratulated on that, but they ought not to be. Bibles are not meant to be locked away in a drawer or wrapped up in paper. They are meant to be read. When you get Bibles as Sunday School prizes, don't keep them good. Do not spoil or mistreat them, but use them. That is what St. Paul meant when he wrote, "For whatever was written in former days was written for our instruction, that by steadfastness and by the encouragement of the scriptures we might have hope." *(Romans 15.4)*

We shall have hope in this life and the life to come if we know the Bible, and if through the Bible we come to know the God and Father of our Lord Jesus Christ as our God and Father too.

------------ · ------------

The penknife

A thing isn't lost, it is said, if you know where it is. In that case, my penknife is not lost. I know exactly where it is, but it might as well be lost for all the good it is to me. It was a penknife I liked. During the holidays, we were having a picnic. I put my penknife down on a little shelf close to the windscreen of my car. It was lying there quite peaceably when someone gave it a knock and it disappeared. Close to the windscreen is a thin slot for the hot air to rise through and demist the windscreen. It is a thin slit, but wide enough for my knife, for down it went.

Well, we searched under the bonnet and behind the dashboard and we unscrewed this and that. We tried fishing with a magnet and with a bent pin. But all to no avail. Somewhere under the windscreen of my car is my nice knife, but for all the use it is to me, it might as well be in China or Peru or on the moon.

Do you have a Bible at home, boys and girls? Of course you have. You know exactly where it is, in the drawer or in the bookcase. But if you don't read it, it might as well be in China or Peru or on the moon.

Do you believe in God? Of course you do. But when last did you pray, really and truly in earnest all by yourself? If you don't pray, there might as well be no God so far as you are concerned.

Are you a Christian? Of course you are. But when did you last think of Christ or ask him to guide you and direct what you say?

It does not matter how real God and Christ and the Bible are, if we pay no attention to them, they might as well not be there.

That is what Moses meant when he said, "Make certain that you do not forget the Lord." *(Deuteronomy 6.12)*

Pen-friends

How do you choose your friends? Usually at first it is by how they look or by the sound of their voice. You either like the look or the sound of a person, or you don't. Recently I met a French lady who has a friend in England whom she has known for many,

many years. They became friends when they were both at school. Now they are both grandmothers and they are friends still. But they have never spoken to each other and they have never once seen each other. They know each other only through the hundreds of letters they have written to each other through the years. They are pen-pals.

So it is possible to have friends whom one has never seen. There are some people I regard as my friends although they have been dead for a long time and I know them only through books which I've read over and over again.

None of us has ever seen God and he hasn't sent us any letters, or at least not through the post. But we can read what he said and what he did in the Bible and come to know him quite well. Above all we can become friends of God through Jesus Christ, for he once said, "You are my friends if you do what I tell you." *(John 15.14)*

WE ALL NEED EACH OTHER

Crazy arithmetic

Are you good at arithmetic, boys and girls? Even if you're not very good at it you probably know the answer to this question, "What do one and one make?" Everybody, even little infants, know that one and one make two. But are you sure, boys and girls?

I'm not. Quite often, for instance, I take one and one, a bride and a bridegroom, and make one. When two people marry they're not separate people any more, they are just like one person. So sometimes one and one make one. Then you've all heard of Dr. Jekyll and Mr. Hyde. He was only one man all the time, but by day he was the good Dr. Jekyll and by night the wicked Mr. Hyde. I've known little boys and girls too who were certainly like two people, a good one and a bad one, a lazy and a quick one, a true and a false one, all boxed up inside one little body and called by one name. That means that sometimes one makes two or even more. Then, we've all seen a crack regiment marching past us, and we've heard people say that they move "like one man." So sometimes one and one make one, sometimes one makes two, and sometimes many people make one! It is all very confusing.

Even here in the church where there are hundreds of us, we join all our voices in one when we sing, and sometimes when we pray together we join our hearts and souls in one too. Throughout the world there are millions and millions of Christians differing in colour and language, and in their ways of worship and of speaking about God, but they are all at one in this, if they are real Christians, in the love of the Lord Jesus Christ.

Remember, the next time you do arithmetic, that there are

exceptions even to its rules, and remember Christ's prayer for those who love him, that "All may be one." *(John 17.21)*

The conductor

Not long ago, boys and girls, I went to hear the famous Vienna Boys' Choir. It was a very moving and thrilling experience. What surprised me, and I think many of those who were there, was that there were only twenty-one members of the choir. I had somehow imagined there would be a very much larger number, and I could hardly credit that this small group could be heard all over the great City Hall in Glasgow where they were singing. But they were heard perfectly. They provided a programme which lasted over two hours and ranged from Purcell to "Auld Lang Syne".

I said there were twenty-one members of the choir and so there were, but only twenty of them sang. The twenty-first did not once open his mouth. Yet he was the most important person on the platform. If one of the others had been off with a cold, we might have noticed it a little, but probably not. If this particular person had been off, the concert would simply not have been possible. Without him the singers would all have been at sixes and sevens, and there would have been nothing but discords and irregularities. You have guessed who the non-singing member of the choir was, I think. He was the conductor. Without a good conductor it is not possible to have a good choir or orchestra. Even in Macnamara's Band, the most important member was not McCafferty who played the big bassoon, nor Cormack who played the horn, but Macnamara who kept them all in order. If every singer in a choir or player on an instrument did just what he or she liked, the result would be dreadful.

And life's like that too. There is nothing but misery if we all go our own roads and do what we like. The only way in which we can live in harmony with each other is if we are all obedient to the same Lord and Master. In that way we shall help and not hurt one another. That is what Jesus meant when he said, "One is your Master, even Christ, and all ye are brethren." *(Matthew 23.8)*

The missing glove

Can you see, boys and girls, what I have in my hand? It's a glove, quite a nice glove. It has no holes in it. It fits me perfectly, but it has no neighbour. I lost the other one a long time ago, and have kept on hoping it would turn up, but it never has. So, for want of a neighbour, this good glove is completely useless.

And what's true of gloves is true of people. We are not much use without our neighbours. The poor man in the parable, who had been attacked by thieves, would have died if the Good Samaritan had not come along, willing to be neighbourly. None of us can manage without other people. Children need parents to look after them, and parents need children to look after, otherwise they wouldn't be parents at all. Patients need the doctor, but equally the doctor needs patients. The butcher needs the baker, and the baker needs the butcher. We all need the farmer to grow our food, the dustman to keep our streets clean, the policeman to keep us safe.

We all need each other and we all need God, who is the Maker and the Father of us all. He has sent us into his world to live together and to help each other as neighbours should, and he has given us his commandment, "Thou shalt love thy neighbour." *(Luke 10.27)*

Together

Girls and boys, I don't have a tiger in my tank, but here in the pulpit I have a quantity of the strongest, most important, most powerful things in the world. Now I shall pick up one of them between my finger and thumb. Do you know what it is? I'll tell you in a moment or two.

But first I'll tell you about a visit I paid not long ago to what is called a hydro-electric scheme. There was a wall of concrete hundreds of yards long and hundreds of feet thick. It was built right across a river so as to form a great artificial lake, a dam as it is called. The water was pouring at a terrific rate through a certain number of holes in the wall and as it ran it made electricity; electricity to light up your homes, and cook your food, and make the railway trains run and do all sorts of wonderful things.

Now do you know what I'm holding between my finger and thumb? It is a drop of water which I picked up from the glass in front of me. It may not be very important or strong all by itself, but together with millions of others it can give all the light and heat and power we need.

You and I may not be very strong or very important all by ourselves, but together with the millions of others who make up the Church we can do all sorts of things to make the world a happier, better, brighter place. But, remember, every drop counts. If in the great hydro-electric scheme one tiny drop of water had said "I'm not joining in, I'll just run away into the ground," and then another, and then another had done the same, there would have been no dam; no power; no electricity. It is all the drops of water *together* which create the power, and every drop counts. Just as every boy and girl, and every man and woman counts, every prayer and every sacrifice in the world-wide, never-ending work of Christ's Church and Kingdom. That is why Christ said "If two or three are gathered *together* in my name, there am I." *(Matthew 18.20)*

The Pow-Wow

I have a friend, boys and girls, who is a Red Indian. He is a chief of the Ponca tribe, and when we were in Oklahoma in the United States, he took us to a great Indian Pow-Wow.

The old men of the tribe beat drums and sang and the young men and women and boys and girls appeared, hundreds of them, from where they had been camping, some in real Indian Tepees, among the trees. They were most beautifully dressed, with gorgeous eagle and wild turkey feather head-dresses. They danced war dances and circle dances and the drums beat louder and the bells on the ankles of the dancers rang out as darkness fell. It was very beautiful and very thrilling.

I had a share in the Pow-Wow too. I didn't have a feather head-dress or even a tomahawk. But before the Pow-Wow started, the Presiding Chief came to me and said that they never began without saying a prayer, and he invited me to lead them. So, then and there, in the open air, surrounded by hundreds of Red Indian braves and squaws in their wonderful costumes, I prayed to the great Father of all.

St. Paul once wrote to the Christians at Corinth, "There is for us only one God, the Father . . . and there is only one Lord Jesus Christ."

God is the Father of white people and black, of Indians and Americans, of Scots and Africans, of Germans and Russians, and there is one saviour of all, Jesus Christ.

The Olympic logo

Do you see what this is, girls and boys? Five circles, all linked up with each other. Together they are the symbol of the Olympic Games.

Why are there five circles and not four or six? The reason is that there are five continents – Europe, Asia, Africa, Australasia and America – which take part in the Games. Sometimes they don't seem to do it particularly well, but the Olympic Games are meant to link up all the five continents, all the people in the world, in friendship. The Games are not only a matter of winning medals, but of winning friends.

We all need each other. At breakfast you maybe drank tea which came from Asia, with sugar in it which came from the West Indies. Perhaps you had butter which came from New Zealand. Your grapefruit or orange juice probably came from Africa. No one continent, no one country can get on very well without all the others.

That is the way God meant it to be. He made of one blood, all nations, made us so that we need each other and can help each other. He made us all and he loves us all, wherever in the world we happen to be born.

All men and women in all of the five continents, all three thousand million of us, are members of the one great family, for there is one God and Father of all, who is Lord of all, works through all, and is in all.

_____ · _____

All together now!

I'm going to ask the organ to give the children's talk today. At least, I'm going to ask the organist to play a hymn for us, but instead of playing all four parts together, I'm going to ask him to play the parts separately.

Listen to this hymn and see if you know which it is. (Organist plays bass line.) Don't you recognise it? Listen to this then. (Organist plays tenor part.) And then listen to this (Alto line.) Now Mr.–, play all the parts together, please.

So what is the hymn? That's right. But it's not any use playing the four parts separately if you are still trying to find out what hymn it is. To sound right they must all be played together.

It is no use if all the members of a family try to get their own way. It is far better when they act together. It is no use if everybody in the church is fighting. It is no use when everybody in the world is trying to go their own way. It is far better if we can all sing our separate songs, and play our separate parts, and do our separate things in harmony with each other, and in obedience to the one God and Father of us all, who is above all, and through all, and in you all.

-------------------   ·   -------------------

Foreign languages

Do you speak many foreign languages, girls and boys? Of course you do. You've just spoken a Hebrew word – "amen." It means "truly." In a minute I'll give out a hymn and that word "hymn" is Greek for "song." When you say that you are going to school, "school" is a Latin word. When you spoke of your pyjamas this morning you were using an Indian word. "Coffee" is Turkish and "tea" is Chinese. English has borrowed words from nearly all the hundreds and hundreds of different languages there are in the world.

But there is one word which is the same in every language and that is the word "Jesus." Jesus was born into the world to be the friend and helper of people everywhere, in every country in the world and speaking every language.

-------------------   ·   -------------------

A three-fold cord

"A three-fold cord is not quickly broken." That's an odd text, boys and girls, but I'll try to show you what it means. When you make a hole in your sock or your pullover, your mother mends it with wool, and here is a piece of wool. Can you all see it? People often say that wool is not nearly so strong as it used to be. Certainly it's quite easy to break it. Look! I've broken it without any trouble at all. If you twine two bits of wool together, it is still possible, but not so easy to break them. With a bit of an effort, however, I've managed it. But here I have plaited three strands of wool together and I just can't break it at all. It's true enough that a three-fold cord is not quickly broken.

And that is what the Church is all about. We could each of us try to worship God and to serve Christ all on our own. If we bind ourselves together, however, as we do in the Church, we are able to help each other to worship God far more effectively. Moreover, we can do far more for Christ and do it better. Some things, like setting up an Eventide Home or sending help to the famine areas of the world or organizing Christian missions, we can do only if we combine with other people.

Although already you are in a sense members of the Church, I hope that you will all become full communicants when you are older. Being confirmed means being made strong for Christ. You will be stronger for being in the Church, and we in the Church will be stronger because you are with us. It is true not only of a three-fold cord, but even more of a mani-fold cord that it is not quickly broken. That is why Christ's last command to his followers was to go into all the world and make disciples of *all* nations. The more strands in the cord, the stronger it is. "A three-fold cord is not quickly broken." *(Ecclesiastes 4.12)*

The hammer and the nail

A long time ago there was a song at the top of the charts which went like this:

> "I'd rather be a hammer than a nail,
> Yes I would,
> If I could,
> I really would."

Which would you rather be – a hammer or a nail?

It might be rather nice to be a hammer and go about hitting things on the head. A nail is no use without a hammer. Still, it might get dull after a while to be always hammering. Perhaps that is why hammers sometimes fly off the handle.

It would be quite nice to be a nail, just to stay in one place and hold things together. Nails are such useful things. Think what would happen if all the nails in the world disappeared. Houses and churches and furniture would all collapse as if made of cards. If a nail is no use without a hammer, a hammer is a pretty useless object without nails for it to knock in. The truth is that the hammer needs the nail and the nail needs the hammer.

So it is with people too. We all need each other: the young need the old and the old need the young; the people who can work with their hands need those who can work with their heads, and the other way about.

That is why we should never look down on people who are different from us, on people whose skin is a different colour from ours, on those who speak differently or those who belong to different churches. We all need each other and we all need God.

Neither a hammer nor a nail is much use unless there is someone who can use them. So it is with us in the various churches. It does not matter that we are different from each other. What does matter is that we, all of us, should be ready to put ourselves into the hand of God, to do what he wants us to do and to be what he means us to be.

Then it won't matter whether you are a hammer or a nail. It won't. It really won't.

LET US PRAY

The cannibal bus

Do you know what a cannibal is? Of course you do. It is someone who, instead of eating steak or chops for his dinner, eats people. At least they used to do that, but our missionaries have done such wonderful work that there are not many left in the world – or so I thought! But a little while ago I met a cannibal, not far away in the South Sea Islands, but right here in Glasgow. It was not a cannibal man I met. It was a cannibal bus!

It just looked ordinary, like any other bus, but when I went inside and sat down, I discovered its terrible secret, for there, just behind the driver, printed in great big letters, I read these words – THIS BUS EATS TWENTY-SIX PASSENGERS. I blinked my eyes and looked again, but I had made no mistake – THIS BUS EATS TWENTY-SIX PASSENGERS. "This is dreadful," I thought to myself, "I wonder if it eats twenty-six passengers every day!" However, I looked round and nobody else seemed to be worrying. Then I saw why. Originally, the notice had read – THIS BUS SEATS TWENTY-SIX PASSENGERS, but some bad person had scraped out the "s" in "seats" with his knife and turned "seats" into "eats." Just by scratching out one single letter he had turned a perfectly ordinary, decent bus into a rampageous cannibal! It just shows how important even one letter can be. It is always the little things in life that count – one little letter, one little word, one little act.

A little word like "please" makes all the difference to life. It is like the drop of oil that makes the wheels go round. People may not notice much if it is there, but they are upset if it is left out.

To say grace at meals does not take long, but if we forget I am sure that God is disappointed that we should take his gifts without saying "Thank you."

To say our prayers does not take long, but we should never forget to pray, for it is through prayer that God gets into our lives. That is why St. Paul asks us not to forget our prayers. Remember what he said – "Pray without ceasing." *(1 Thessalonians 5.17)*

Wait for an answer

The other evening I went to call on a lady who is a member of my congregation and who lives in a block of flats. I rang the doorbell. As there seemed to be no answer I decided that she could not be at home, and started to walk down the stairs. I had not gone very far, however, when the door was hastily opened and, to my great astonishment, I heard the lady of the house say, "You wee rascal, I'll . . ." and then she saw me and stopped. What she was going to do to the wee rascal I shall never know. I went back, of course, and the poor lady was all confusion and apologies. It seems that some bad boys had been ringing her doorbell and then running away to tease her. When she found nobody at the door, she had thought it was the same boys, and spoke before taking time to see who it was. It is a silly game, to ring doorbells and run. It makes grown-ups cross and unhappy needlessly. There is no point in summoning someone unless you wait for an answer.

But of course, that is what we sometimes do to God. We say a word or two of prayer, but we don't wait for an answer. We are up from our knees and doing something else or going somewhere else without even listening to hear what he has to say to us. That is not much use. We must take time for our prayers and really wait on God. Only so shall we find the truth of Isaiah's promise, "Then shalt thou call, and the Lord shall answer." *(Isaiah 58.9)*

Pray always

Last Sunday, a little boy came to a certain church for the very first time. He sat beside his daddy as good as gold. Presently, when the minister said "Let us pray," his father said to him, "Now, clasp your hands and close your eyes." Do you know what the little boy said then? "Why should I? I am not in bed." Obviously, he was a well-brought-up little boy who was taught to say his prayers last thing at night, and that is a very good thing.

He was quite wrong, however, in thinking that you can never say your prayers at any other time. God is just as ready to listen to us first thing in the morning as at night, just as happy to speak with us on a weekday as on a Sunday. He is always far more ready to hear us than we are to pray, and accustomed to give far more than either we ask or deserve. So don't let us ration our prayers or keep them for just one time or place. "Pray at all times." *(Ephesians 6.18) (R.S.V.)*

Perth and earth

Sometimes ministers tell stories which they have just made up themselves, but here is one that really happened. It is about a little girl who lives in Dunblane where I live, and that is in Perthshire in Scotland. She is not a very big girl. She is much too young to come to church, but her mother has taught her to say the Lord's Prayer. At least she thought she had. But the other evening as she was listening to her daughter saying her prayers, this is what she heard. "Our Father which art in Heaven, hallowed be Thy name. Thy Kingdom come." Well, that was all right, but not the next words, for they were, "Thy will be done in Perth as it is in Heaven." That is not what Jesus taught his disciples to say. I don't suppose when he lived on earth he had ever heard of Perthshire.

What he did say, of course, was "Thy will be done in earth as it is in Heaven."

Yet the little girl's prayer was a very good prayer, which we could all pray, putting in the name of our own home town instead of Perth. "Thy will be done in Glasgow, or London, or New York, as it is in Heaven." We should also say, "Thy will be done in our house and in my life." We must learn to say that prayer and mean it, if the will of God is to be done in Perth, in Britain, and in all the world for which Christ died.

———————— · ————————

Bedtime prayers

The other day I read a story, a true story, about a princess. She was called Princess Marina and she was our Queen's aunt.

When she was a little girl, she was like lots of other girls and boys, she didn't like going to bed early and she thought up all sorts of excuses for staying up. One night she was terribly keen to stay up, and you'll never guess what her excuse was? You can try it yourself, if you like, one of these nights. When she was told it was time for her to go to bed, she said, "Not yet. Lots and lots of boys and girls are going to bed at this time. God must be terribly busy listening to the prayers of children all over the world. I'll just wait till the rush is over and God will have more time to listen to me."

Well, it was a good try, but it didn't work. God is never too busy to listen to the prayers of any one of his children. In a wonderful way, he pays as much attention to each of us as if there were nobody else to heed in the world, just as he loves each of us as if there were but one person in all the world to love.

No matter how many people are saying their prayers at the same time, God hears your prayer.

The God of patience

There is a little girl I know quite well who, like a good girl, says her prayers every night. Usually she says them quite slowly and clearly. One night she got to the middle of her prayer and then she rushed through the last words. When she said, "Amen," she added, "Excuse me for hurrying, God, but I thought I was going to cough."

I'm sure God does understand if sometimes we hurry our prayer a bit or nearly fall asleep.

But God is never in a hurry with us. He waits till we have finished speaking, listens to every word we have to say. He never falls asleep while we are talking to him. As he showed us in Jesus, God is wonderfully patient, which is why St. Paul calls him, "A God of patience." *(Romans 15.5)*

_____ · _____

The Red Indian Princess

What do you speak with, boys and girls? "Well," you say, "that's easy – with our mouths." Is that the only way in which you can speak to people? I don't think so. For example, when you want someone to be very quiet, you don't need to say anything. You just put your fingers to your lips. To beckon with your finger means "Come here"; a hand behind the ear means "Speak up." If you want to be cheeky, you stick out your tongue. We all use sign language, don't we?

When you go home today, make a list of all the signs you use and see if you can tell a story without speaking a word.

Do you remember me telling you about the Red Indian Pow-Wow last week? Well, after I had said the prayer at the beginning of it all, a beautiful princess appeared and she led us in the Lord's Prayer, but she led us without saying a word. Using only her hands, she showed us by gestures what the Lord's Prayer meant – rather as a minister to deaf people does. It was a sort of acted prayer. It was very beautiful and very touching.

You know, boys and girls, it is not a bad idea to act out your prayers. If you ask God to let you pass your exams, then go and do some studying. If you pray for old people, go and do something for some old person you know. If you pray for peace, stop quarrelling with your brother. If you ask God to bless your father and mother, show him you mean it by being kind and helpful to them yourself.

Remember the Red Indian Princess and her acted prayer. Don't say a prayer unless you act on it too.

———————— · ————————

The boy who trusted

In Switzerland, quite near Lucerne, there is a little town called Altdorf. In the square at Altdorf is a statue to somebody you've all heard of – William Tell. You know the story, don't you? William Tell refused to recognise the foreign tyrant who had conquered the part of Switzerland where he lived. He was arrested and was told that he would be set free only if he shot at an apple on the head of his little son. The apple was placed on the boy's head. William Tell took aim. The arrow flew from the bow. It split the apple in two, but did not even graze the boy's head.

It's a great story, but one thing about it has always worried me. I think the statue should have been put up, not to William Tell, but to his son. It was he who was the real hero, for it was he who had the courage to face a terrible death from the speeding arrow. It was he who had such complete trust and confidence in his father that he did not flinch when he saw him draw the bow and take aim.

A friend of mine once tried to learn how to use a real grown-up bow and arrow in Holyrood Park in Edinburgh. He didn't hit the bull's eye. He didn't even hit the target. His arrow landed right on the roof of Holyrood Palace. *His* son would be very foolish to let him try to hit an apple perched on his head. Not many fathers could do much better.

Perhaps it does not matter whether or not you can trust your father as an archer, so long as you can trust him in the more important things in life. I am sure you can, for you know that he will do all he can to help you and nothing to do you harm.

The message of the Bible is that God is like the best and wisest and most loving father who can be imagined. We can trust him completely and for ever, without any trace of doubt or fear.

That is why, when Jesus taught his disciples to pray, he told them to begin, "Our Father." *(Matthew 6.9)*

Stop talking

Last Sunday a little girl, we'll call her Carol, came to church. She is only three years old, and this was her first time there. Her parents are very good parents and they had told her how to behave in church. Well, Carol was as good as gold all the time she was there except that when I was saying a prayer, she said something, not once, but several times. She said it in a small voice which I could hear, and so could her father and mother, but nobody else. Do you know what she said? "Mr. Gray, stop talking. Mr. Gray, stop talking."

Well, she's such a well-brought-up little girl that I could hardly believe my ears. After church, I said to her, "Carol, why did you keep on saying 'Stop talking'?" Do you know what her answer was? "It's very rude to talk in church."

Of course, she was right. It is very rude to talk in church if you're just chatting to your neighbour about school or football or television.

But it is not a bit rude to talk to God or to listen for him to speak. For that is all prayer means. It is talking to God. There is a time and a place to speak; and a time and a place to listen; a time to sing and a time to pray.

One thing we can be quite sure of is that God is always ready to listen when we speak, wherever we are or whoever we are.

―――――――――― · ――――――――――

The tube of toothpaste

I'm going to do something now which I did once already this morning, and you've all done it this morning too. You took a tube of toothpaste in your hand and you squeezed some out. Rather fun.

Well, that's easy enough. I can do that too. But I'll tell you what you can't do, what nobody can do, and that is get it back in the tube again. Like Humpty Dumpty who could not be put together again by all the King's horses and all the King's men. It is easy to do but very hard to undo.

That is true of a lot of things. It is easy to tell a lie, or to say something unkind. It is impossible to un-say it. It is easy to do something cruel, but difficult to un-do it.

That is why, day by day and hour by hour, we need the help of the Lord Jesus Christ, so as not to say or do things we wish we'd never said or done. Jesus is a very wonderful Master and even when we do go wrong and make a mess of things, he's willing to help us clear up the mess we've made and to start afresh.

That's what we are asking him to do when we pray "Forgive us our debts."

―――――――――― · ――――――――――

Prayers God doesn't answer

The other day I heard a story about a little girl who was being very naughty. It seems that the people who live next door to her very often take her with them on a picnic. On this particular day, however, she hadn't been asked. As soon as she saw the preparations for the picnic being made she started to cry, and cried solidly all through breakfast. After a while the kind neighbours actually heard her. Taking pity, they came in and said she might come. As soon as she heard that, she cried all the louder. At this, her mother quite lost patience with her. "You cried when you weren't going on the picnic," she said, "and now you cry because you are. What *is* the matter with you?" To which, through her tears, the little girl replied, "It's too late for them to ask me now. I've prayed for rain." Well, of course, fortunately for her God wouldn't hear that prayer; or rather, wouldn't answer it. He never does answer us when we ask for bad things. Indeed, he only gives us the sort of things which we can ask for in the name of Christ, the sort of things which Christ himself loves to give. That's why Christ said, "Whatsoever ye shall ask *in my name*, that will I do." *(John 14.13)*

———————— · ————————

The hungry swans

Next to the very beautiful Cathedral of Wells, there is a palace where the Bishop lives. It is a very old palace, more like a castle really, for all round about it there is water. You know what that is called – a moat. There is a bridge across the moat and just at the side of the bridge there is a bell with a long chain attached to it. The chain hangs down almost to the water, where nobody could reach it – nobody, that is, except some swans swimming up and down in the moat. It is the swans who ring the bell. When they are hungry, they catch the chain in their beaks and give it a pull. When the bell rings, people know that the swans are hungry and bring food to feed them. It is the swans' way of saying "Please."

I knew some children once who were apt to say "I *want* breakfast," or "I *want* more pudding," or "I *want* a sweetie." When they said that, their mother always said, "I want gets nothing" – and nothing was what they got until they said, "Please may I have."

Well, it is very important that we should learn good manners, learn to be polite, especially to our parents and the people we live with. We should never take people for granted.

Nor should we take God for granted. He is very good to us, he has given us life and health and food and laughter and so much else. The least we can do is to say, "Please" and "Thank you" to him, which is just what we do when we obey the Bible when it says, "Praise the Lord . . . , and do not forget how kind he is." *(Psalm 103.2)*

Saint Bean

Have you ever heard of St. Bean? When a friend told me about him I thought he was teasing me and would tell me next that St. Bean's first name was Heinz! But apparently St. Bean was a real man who came from Ireland many years ago to preach in Perthshire. Everybody with the name Bean or McBean, McVean or Methven can claim a link with St. Bean.

The beautiful little church of Fowlis Wester near Crieff is called after St. Bean. When a former minister of Fowlis Wester heard that the fourth man to land on the moon was called Alan Bean and that he was a very good Christian and Sunday School teacher, he wrote to him. Alan Bean wrote back and said that one day he would try to find his way to Fowlis Wester. You would think he wouldn't have too much trouble in doing so, since he'd found his way to the moon.

When Alan Bean went to the moon he took with him a piece of McBean tartan, specially woven in Forfar, and he brought it back home again. He sent a bit of this tartan to the minister of Fowlis Wester. The next time you are up that way, ask to be taken to the lovely church of Fowlis Wester and there you'll see a bit of tartan which has been to the moon and back – a very far-travelled bit of tartan indeed.

But you know, there are wonderful things in your own home too. You've probably seen television pictures which have come from the other side of the world or even from space. Even if you haven't, you can look out any night and see the light which has come all the way from the moon to shine in at your bedroom window. At this very moment you can see something which has come from much further than even that. The sunshine has come all of ninety-three million miles to light up the church today.

What you did a few minutes ago was even more wonderful. You joined in the Lord's Prayer, and if you did so sincerely and honestly, then you words reached the heart of God in an instant and at once there came back from God some of the blessing for which we asked.

We are really very silly if we neglect the marvellous power God has given us to speak with him, for he has promised "While they are yet speaking, I will hear." *(Isaiah 65.24)*

The ill shop

About ten miles from here there is a little town which you all know. Right in the middle of the main street there is a shop, and above the door is a sign. Do you know what it says? "The Ill

Shop." You would not imagine that that sort of shop would get much trade. I cannot think that anybody would go in and buy a week of flu, or a little common cold, or two yards of tummy-ache. Surely there is enough illness in the world without anyone having to go and buy more.

I was just deciding that the people in the shop must be very strange people indeed, when I looked again and saw that originally the notice had read "THE MILL SHOP." Somehow the one letter "M" had fallen off and so the very sensible and useful "MILL SHOP" had become the very evil and sinister "ILL SHOP."

It just shows how important a single letter is.

A prayer doesn't take long and it does not seem to matter much, but if you miss out your prayers, then your whole day becomes sick. One hour a week in church may not appear to be very important, but it can make the difference between a dull, useless life and a good and happy one, a little like the life of Christ.

Little things, one letter in a shop sign, a daily prayer, or weekly worship can make all the difference. As St. Paul said, "Never stop praying." *(1 Thessalonians 5.17)*

NO ONE HAS EVER SEEN GOD

The invisible God

On a fine day recently when the sky was blue and clear, there were four aeroplanes, all jets, performing the most complicated manoeuvres just over the city where I live. Mark you, I didn't see them, they were much too high up for that. I couldn't hear them; for all around me was the roar of Glasgow's traffic, of buses and trains and cars. I could neither see nor hear the planes, but I knew that they were there. How, boys and girls? Well, you have probably guessed already. All over the blue sky, like a network of lace, were the lovely white patterns we call vapour trails. We know that wherever there are those white vapour trails, there are aeroplanes. So, although we may not be able to see or hear the aeroplanes, we know that they are there – high up in the sky – by the signs of their presence that they leave behind.

Now there are some foolish people who say that there is no God, just because they can't see or hear him. It is true, as St. Paul says, that our God is "the invisible God"; but he has given all sorts of signs of his presence. Look at the perfection of a flower or the glory of the sky and of the sea! Think about the love which has surrounded you since you were a tiny baby! These are the signs of God, and he has not left himself without a witness, the New Testament says, and neither he has. Although we've never seen him, we know by these things that he is not far away from any one of us. Through Jesus he has come closest of all, for we can see shining through the words and the life after death and the rising of Jesus Christ, the glory of the Father, the glory of "the invisible God." *(Colossians 1.15)*

The hidden God

"Twinkle, twinkle, little star,
How I wonder what you are
Up above the world so high
Like a diamond in the sky."

That's a poem we all learn, boys and girls, when we are little, and it is a poem we never forget. Every time we go out after dark and look up and see the stars we are reminded of it. And we should often take time to look up into the night sky, for stars are lovely things.

One night when I was leaving a friend's house I looked up and somewhat sadly said, "There are no stars tonight." "You're wrong," said my friend, "there are lots of them, just as many as ever, thousands upon thousands. It is just that we cannot see them." He was right, of course. Often, in the city especially, smoke or fog or low clouds hide the stars from us completely, but they are there just the same.

It is good to know that that is true; that the stars are always twinkling away up in the sky – even when we can see nothing but inky blackness. It is true equally of God. Sometimes clouds of pride or anger, the smoke of our battles, the fog of our silliness, hide God from us. But he is there just the same behind the clouds. He is there always, even when you and I cannot see him.

"Lo, he goeth by me," said Job, "and I see him not." *(Job 9.11)*

———————— · ————————

Make a space for God

Do you know what an atheist is, boys and girls? It is somebody who says that there is no God. We should all be sorry for someone who is so mistaken. I heard of an atheist who was not a bit sorry to be an atheist. Indeed, he was rather proud of it. He even made a great big poster which he stuck up in his office and this is how it read:

GOD IS NOWHERE

One day a friend who was not an atheist came in to see him. He rather surprised the atheist by saying, "I like your poster, and I don't want to change a single word or a single letter, but I would like to make a little space where you have none." So he took the poster down and he didn't change a single word or a single letter, but right in the middle of NOWHERE he made a little space. Then he put the poster up again. Where it had once read GOD IS NOWHERE, it now read:

GOD IS NOW HERE

Sometimes it seems that God is nowhere, but if we make a little space for him every night by saying our prayers and by coming to church on Sunday, we shall find that God is now here. I think that is what the writer of the Psalm meant when he wrote, "Be still and know that I am God." *(Psalm 46.10)*

A mountain through a pin-hole

I can see all your faces, girls and boys; nice, clean, bright and shining faces they are. And you can see my face. If, however, I put this sheet of paper right in front of my face, you cannot see me any more. But I can still see you. For in the middle of the sheet of paper I have made a hole with a pin, and even though it is a tiny hole, looking through it I can see you all. Later on you must try it for yourself. From a suitable distance you can actually see through the pin-hole something as big as the Cathedral, even a distant mountain. It's astonishing, if you think of it. Obviously the mountain is on one side of the paper, yet somehow it is able to reach through the tiny pin-hole to your eye on the other side. If you want to have it explained, you must ask your father, and if he can't tell you, ask your teacher tomorrow. But don't ask me, for I don't know how it happens. All I know is that it does happen and that it is rather wonderful.

There is something even more wonderful, and it is this. God is very, very great. None of us can see him, at least not face to face. Yet he has let us see what he is like in the one human life of Jesus of Nazareth. As we read about what Jesus said and what Jesus did, we can look through that one short life and see quite clearly the greatness and goodness and glory of God. That's what St. John meant when once he said, "No one has ever seen God. The only Son . . . has made him known." That is what Jesus meant when he said, "He that hath seen me hath seen the Father." *(John 14.9)*

Parachutes

Have you ever seen free-fall parachuting? I watched five soldiers doing it the other day. It was a wonderful thing to see them, just tiny dots in the sky falling at one hundred and eighty miles per hour and then, just at the right moment, they pulled the ripcords of their huge, multicoloured parachutes and came down more and more slowly till they landed safe and well with hardly a bump.

It was all very wonderful, but thinking about it, the two most wonderful things were the force which pulled their parachutes towards the ground and the other force which gradually slowed them down.

You might say that it was just their own weight which pulled them down, but of course they would have had no weight but for the pull of the mysterious force of the earth called gravity.

You might say that it was their parachutes which kept them from falling to the ground too quickly, but that would not be true. If you drop a parachute from a plane it will fall like a stone unless, and until, it fills with air.

Both the force which pulled the parachutists down, gravity, and the power which slowed them down, air, are invisible, like most of the important things in life. Nobody has ever seen the really important things like love and truth and goodness.

And nobody has ever seen the most important person of all, the person who made us, and loves us, and wants us to be with him for ever. Nobody has ever seen him, but he is real just the same, he is simply "the invisible God." *(Colossians 1.15)*

WHAT CAN LITTLE HANDS DO?

Put your whole self in

I'm not magic, girls and boys, but I am fairly sure I know of two questions your mother asked before you left for church. The first was, "Do you have your collection?" The second was, "Do you have a hankie?"

There is a girl I know. Though she is only five, she goes to church every Sunday. One Sunday, as she was leaving the house, her mother said, "Joanna, do you have your collection?" And Joanna said, "Yes." Her mother said, "Do you have a hankie?" And Joanna said, "No." So her mother asked, "What will you do if your nose runs?" And Joanna said, "I'll run after it."

It sounds rather fun – a nose running away on its own little legs and its owner running after it, trying hard to catch up. But, of course, it couldn't happen. Where you go, your nose goes too, and where your nose goes, you've got to go. However much it may run, it can't run away from you, nor you from it.

When you dance the Hokey Cokey, you say or sing, "Put your right hand in," then "Put your left hand in," then it is your right foot, then your left, then your ear, then your nose. But that can't happen in real life. You can't split yourself up and let one part of you do one thing and another part of you do something else. Sometimes people try. They try to do their homework and watch television. It's not usually a success. Sometimes they try to eat sweets and sing. That's not a success either. You can't really put a part of yourself into anything, least of all into your service of Christ. If we are going to make our lives fine and good, like his, we have got to put our whole selves into his service, holding nothing back. He held nothing back from us.

———————— · ————————

191

St J— 1965

The Prime Minister

A certain little girl went home and said, "Do you know who was in our school today? The Prime Minister!" "Mrs. Thatcher?" "No, Mr. Gray."

We can't all be Prime Minister. We can't all be Ministers in the Church. But we can all be ministers – women and men and girls and boys. For "minister" just means "a servant."

We can all serve and obey and follow and love Christ. If we do, we shall all be Christ's ministers or servants.

————————— · —————————

S.O.E.

Do you know who is the kindest, most generous, hardest-working person in the whole world? I do, and I'll tell you the name of the person in a little while, but I'll tell you the person's initials now and see if you can guess who it is. His, or it may be her, initials are S.O.E.

If dishes need to be washed, S.O.E. will wash them. If coal needs to be brought in, S.O.E. will bring it in. If there are errands to be done, S.O.E. will do them. S.O.E. will wash the car at the drop of a hat. If weeds need to be pulled out, S.O.E. will pull them out. If the church needs money, S.O.E. will give it. For any job that needs to be done, for any gift that needs to be made, you can depend on S.O.E.

Do you know what S.O.E. stands for? Some One Else.

It is rather a shame how we leave all the work, all the sacrifices, all the giving, to S.O.E. – to someone else.

Next time some help is needed, some gift is wanted, some job is crying out to be done, let's have pity on poor S.O.E. Instead of saying "Let someone else do it," say "Let me do it."

Long ago when God wanted a message to be taken, he asked,

"Who will go for me?" Isaiah the prophet might have said, "Here is someone else, send him." Instead he said, "Here am I, send me." *(Isaiah 6.8)*

———————— · ————————

The hands of Christ

You have all probably seen a copy of Durer's great picture "Praying Hands". The other day I read in an American book something I didn't know before. The hands are not just anyone's hands. They are the hands of one of Durer's friends, who also wanted to be an artist. So that Durer could have the opportunity to study, his friend gave up his career, and went to work in the fields. With the hard labour, his hands became stiff and coarse, and incapable of fine work. But Durer loved his friend and was grateful for the sacrifice he had made, so he painted the hands, by the labour of which his own career had been made possible. In the broken nails and swollen joints, Durer saw the proof of his friend's love and self-sacrifice.

There's a pair of hands in your home. Once they were white and soft. Now, despite what the soap advertisements on television may say, they're a wee bit rough and red and worn. You know whose hands they are – your Mother's. When you go home, just look at those hands, notice every scar, every bit of roughness and redness, for these things are the proof of your Mother's love.

There's another pair of hands we should often think about, the hands of Christ. They were pierced by nails on a cross, because he loved you and me and all men. But his love was stronger than death. So when he rose from the dead, he came to his friends, and, as if to prove his love for them, "he showed unto them his hands." *(John 20.20)*

Christ without hands

In Germany there is a city called Strasbourg. During the war a church in Strasbourg was destroyed by bombing. At first the people thought that nothing was left of the church but a heap of rubble, but when they began to clear away the rubbish they found a statue of Christ. It was covered with dust but it was unharmed except for one thing. Both hands had been broken off. They searched everywhere but they could not find them. So when the church was rebuilt after the war was over, the statue was re-erected but still without hands.

One day someone made an offer to the minister of the church to have the statue made perfect again by having the hands replaced. The minister and the leaders of the church met to talk about it. Finally they decided to thank the man who had offered to replace the hands, but to say, "No" to his offer.

It was rather a wonderful reason they gave for refusing the offer. The minister said, "So long as the statue of Christ stands complete, but with no hands, people may remember that Christ *has* no hands to do his work in the world except our hands, the hands of ordinary men and women and boys and girls."

All sorts of people need to be helped. Hungry people need to be fed. Sick people need to be nursed. If Christ is to help them he needs the hands of all who love him. Sometimes when there's a big job to be done, people say, "Lend a hand, please." That is what Christ says to us all. "Lend me your hands, both of them, to do my work in the world." Show me how many hands Christ can have in this church this morning.

———————— · ————————

The words are from
Strasbourg Ag ville.

Glue, grit, jelly and soup

A very clever professor at Glasgow University published a book some time ago in which he said that these bodies of ours are made up of four things – glue, grit, jelly and soup. The grit glued together makes bones, our muscles are jelly and our blood a kind of soup. It doesn't sound very nice, does it? But it isn't very different from what the Bible says. "God formed man of the dust of the ground and breathed into his nostrils the breath of life."

It is the breath of life which is the hard bit. Even though you had tons of grit and glue, jelly and soup, you could work away for a million years and all you could make, even if you were very clever, would be a kind of doll, not a human being at all.

Anyway, what matters is not what we're made of, but what we're made for. This morning at breakfast you didn't look to see what kind of china the plates and cups were made out of, nor what kind of metal was used for the spoons. All you were interested in was using them to eat your breakfast. So it doesn't really matter that you and I are made of grit, glue, jelly and soup. What does matter is what we do with our bodies. St. Paul once said, "Your bodies are the temples of the Holy Spirit." So, offer your bodies to God, for that will delight God's heart.

Spring cleaning

One morning quite soon you and I are going to be wakened early. We shall find the carpets rolled up, and the loose-covers off the chairs, and half the furniture in the garden. Spring cleaning will have begun.

When it does begin I always remember the same story. It is a true story, and a sad story, about spring cleaning in a house I once knew. Two ladies had lived in this house for many years. One spring when they were cleaning, one lady said to the other, "What is this brown paper parcel on top of the wardrobe?" The other said "I don't know. For years I've taken it down, dusted it and put it up again. I thought it belonged to you." The first lady said "I thought it was something of yours." So they undid the string and opened the parcel and found a lovely two-pound box of chocolates. But when they opened the box, the chocolates had gone all white and funny and horrid. They sat down and thought about it, and then one of them remembered that years and years before she had been given the box at Christmas and had put it on top of the wardrobe to be safe from her little boys (who were now grown men) and she had forgotten all about it.

The moral of this story is – eat chocolates whenever you get them! There is something in that, but it is true of other gifts too. God has given us all sorts of gifts, hands to serve him, voices with which to praise him, hearts to love him. But if we don't use our gifts they will spoil, just like the chocolates.

That is what St. Paul meant when he said to Timothy, "Stir into flame the gift of God which is within you." *(2 Timothy 1.6)*

Lending a hand

Shakespeare wrote, "Neither a borrower nor a lender be, for loan oft loses both itself and friend." That is good advice. Nothing is more likely to make you lose friends than to start lending to them or borrowing from them. Yesterday, however, I was asked to lend something, and I did. Two men were trying to move a great lump of iron – a lamp post actually. They could not manage it by themselves, so I was asked to lend them something. What do you think it was? You're right. It was a hand.

They did not, of course, mean me to pull off one of my hands and throw it to them, saying "Mind you let me have it back."

That would not be very easy. In fact, if you lend a hand, you've got to lend yourself with it.

There are a great many things God wants to have done in the world, a great many people he wants us to help – people next door, people round the corner and people on the other side of the world. But even God can only do all the things he wants to do if we lend him a hand. When we lend him our hands, we must lend him our hearts too and our whole selves. That is what the Bible means when it says, "Whatsoever thy hand findeth to do, do it with all thy might." *(Ecclesiastes 9.10)*

John o' Groat's House

In some parts of Scotland, when it is raining very hard and the children want it to be fine, they sing this little nursery rhyme:

"Rainey, Rainey, rattle staney,
Don't rain on me.
Rain on John o' Groat's House,
Far ayont the sea."

John o' Groat's House is not really far beyond the sea, but it is right in the north of Scotland, almost in the sea. It got its name from John o' Groat, or John de Groot, a Dutchman, who came to Scotland to live in the time of King James IV. All went well for him and he had eight sons. They all married and had homes of their own. Every year, however, they met on the anniversary of the day when they had first arrived in Scotland.

One year, they all started quarrelling as to who should be "The Boss" and sit at the top of the table. They appealed to their father to settle the matter. John o' Groat said, "Come back next year and I'll tell you. When they came back, they found that the old man had built a room with eight sides to it, and in it a table with eight sides. There was no top or bottom of the table, so there was nothing for them to quarrel about. All eight were equal and none of them was chief. Wasn't that clever?

Jesus had a better way of telling who should be chief. He said, "He that is greatest among you shall be your servant." And to show that he meant it, he himself once took a towel and a basin of water and washed his disciples' feet.

If you and I want to be like Christ, who was the greatest of all, we must learn not to boss and bully each other, but to help and serve each other in love. True greatness is not shown by our wealth, nor by our power, but by our willing service. Jesus said, "He that is greatest among you shall be your servant." *(Matthew 23.11)*

———————— · ————————

Hearts need hands

What is the most important part of your bodies, boys and girls? Some greedy boys might say the tummy, and some vain girls might say the face. But most of us would agree that it was the heart. There it is, right in the middle of our bodies, ceaselessly pumping our blood into every part of us. That is why, when we love somebody, we say we love them with all our hearts.

But, you know, the heart is not much use by itself. If we met a heart walking down the street all by itself one day, looking a little like Humpty Dumpty, we'd give it a good scolding and say, "Go right home and get your body on and your head on top and your arms and legs too."

Once I saw a notice board outside a church with just three words on it. This is what it said: "Hearts need hands." That is true. It is no use to love somebody with your heart unless you show your love by what you do with your hands. Hearts need hands, and eyes too to see what needs doing, and feet to go where help is wanted, and lips to speak words of truth and kindness. Hearts need hands and eyes and feet and lips. "Let us lift up our heart with our hands to God." *(Lamentations 3.41)*

D.I.Y.

Are you good at knowing what initials stand for, boys and girls? I'm sure you know that B.B.C. means British Broadcasting Corporation. R.S.V.P. at the foot of an invitation means "répondez, s'il vous plaît," or "you'd jolly well better send a reply." You know what P.T.O. stands for, please turn over. But the meaning of some initials is not so easy to guess. Recently I saw a shop, and over the door were just three letters – D.I.Y. The shop was selling things like nails, plywood and paint, but it took me a while to puzzle out that the three letters stood for "Do It Yourself."

That is a very good motto for us all. When dishes need washing or coal is wanted for the fire, don't stick your nose in a book and hope that somebody else will wash the dishes or bring in the coal. D.I.Y. Do It Yourself. When some old person needs visiting, don't leave it to the people who are good at that kind of thing. Do It Yourself. When money is wanted for refugees or homeless people, don't let somebody else give it. Do It Yourself. When Christ wants someone to do his work in the world, don't leave it to others. Do It Yourself.

Isaiah tells us that once, long ago, God asked, "Whom shall I send, and who will go for us?" Isaiah did not say, "Let somebody else go. There's so and so or that other person." He said, "Here am I; send me." *(Isaiah 6.8)*

BY THIS SHALL EVERYONE KNOW

The Battle Ensign

Some months ago I spent some time in an aircraft carrier. One day a particularly big flag was needed to decorate the ship, and someone suggested that we try to borrow the Battle Ensign. When I asked why we should use the Battle Ensign for such a peaceful purpose, I was told that it was far and away the biggest flag on any of Her Majesty's ships of war. And you know why that should be so, don't you? In the noise of a naval engagement, amidst all the smoke and confusion, the ships of the Royal Navy fly this huge flag that all may know, friend and enemy alike, whose ships they are and whom they serve. That, too, was what uniform was for, at least at first, that all might know whose side a soldier was on.

There is no uniform for God's army, for the soldiers of Christ, but if we really belong to it we will want people to know. And they will know, not so much by how we look, but by what we say and how we behave. Even although we do not very often speak of Christ, if we are kind and cheerful and true, people will know that we are "on the Lord's side." *(Exodus 32.26).*

Badges

Long ago, poor people were not well looked after. In order to live at all, they often had to beg for money and food from door to door. They were not even allowed to beg unless they wore a badge. In many museums they have selections of Beggars' Badges from all over Scotland. Some are in pewter and some in brass. Some are as large as the palm of your hand.

Well, we don't need to wear Beggars' Badges any more, but a great many people still wear badges of one kind or another. Some people wear Red Cross badges to show, not that they need help, but that they are ready to give help to the sick, the wounded, and the needy in every land on earth. The Boys' and Girls' Brigades, the Guides and the Scouts all have badges. Even I wear a badge most of the time. I wear it round my neck. It is, of course, a clerical collar. No matter where I go, people know that I am a minister.

Christ once said all his followers should wear a badge, so that everybody could recognize them wherever they went. This is what he said: "By this shall everyone know that you are my disciples, if you love one another."

Love is the badge of Christians – love of your own friends and family, love of those who are in need or pain, love of God who first loved us and gave himself for us.

What is your tartan?

Do you have a school uniform? I'm sure you do and that you are very proud of it. Recently I visited a school for boys in Scotland at which the uniform is a little unusual. All the boys wear the same kind of jacket, stockings and cap, and they all wear kilts, but in one way they are all different, for the kilts they wear are of all sorts of different tartans in accordance with the clans to which they belong. If I had known a little more about the various tartans I could have looked at a boy and known right away that he was a Stewart, or a Graham, or a Campbell, or a Buchanan. Originally, of course, that was what tartan was for, so that friend and foe alike might know to which clan the Highlander belonged. I felt quite envious of the boys in their nice kilts. Those of us who don't belong to any clan have just to wear any colour that happens to be available. The colour of our clothes does not tell people anything about us, or at least not our names.

There are some things, of course, they can tell just by looking at us. They can tell, very often, who our fathers and mothers are, at least if we resemble them. Sometimes they can tell what country we come from by our clothes; you might be able to recognize a French boy by his beret, and so on. Most important of all, it is not too hard to know if we are real Christians or not. If we are, if we really are Christ's boys and girls, we shall be truer, kinder, braver, more cheerful than others. These things are the uniform of Christ's soldiers and, if we wear it, people will take knowledge of us, as they did of Peter and John, that we have "been with Jesus." *(Acts 4.13)*

———————— · ————————

Liverymen of Christ

The other day I called at a house where two young girls live. As soon as I rang the doorbell, the younger girl came and looked through the glass door and I heard her say, "Mummy, it's a man." But her big sister came just behind her. She knew better. She said, "It's not a man. It's the minister." It's easy to recognize a minister when you see one. He wears a funny collar and no tie. That is his uniform.

Once upon a time every job had its uniform, its own livery, as it was called. Every master had to give his assistants their proper livery. Then you could just glance at someone and say right away that he was a Grocer, or a Draper, or a Fishmonger, or a Goldsmith, or a Skinner, or a Haberdasher, or a Salter, or an Ironmonger, or a Vintner, or a Clothworker, or a Dyer.

You can't do that nowadays, except for a few people like the policeman, the butcher with his striped apron, and the minister.

But there is one thing you can tell about people pretty easily, and that is whether they're Christians or not. Here is one uniform, one livery, we can all wear – the uniform of Christ's men and women, Christ's boys and girls. What is it? "The girdle of truth, the breastplate of righteousness, the shoes of peace, the shield of faith, the helmet of salvation, the sword of the Spirit." *(from Ephesians 6.14-17)*

By our courage and kindliness, by our cheerfulness and honesty, we can show that we are the Liverymen of Christ.

JESUS OUR MODEL

Carbon paper

Do you ever try to do two things at once? It's not easy. Try patting your head with one hand and rubbing your tummy with the other. But you know, every week I do three things at the same time. I write three letters to my three sons who all live far away now. How do I do it? I could, I suppose, try to write one letter with each hand and write another with a pencil in my teeth, but I don't think it would work.

Actually the secret is this. I type just one letter and have two other sheets of paper underneath, and between each sheet I put a sheet of this stuff – it's called carbon paper. Sometimes my typewriter doesn't spell too well. If I type the wrong thing on the top copy, the other two copies are wrong too. If I get the top copy right, the other two are right also.

You know, it's not only when we are typing letters that we are taking copies. We are copying other people all the time. That's how, when you were very little, you learned to walk and talk and to eat and to dress. When we grow up we learn how to play games and how to drive a car. All by copying other people.

Since in so many things we are copying someone else, it is terribly important that we should get the right person to copy. To help us to get life just right, God sent Jesus into the world, and the more our lives are copies of the life of Jesus, the happier, the better, the more useful they will be.

Jesus once said, "I have set an example for you, so that you may do as I have done." *(John 13.15)*

Funny faces

Do you ever make funny faces, girls and boys? It is not a very nice thing to do – to stick out your tongue, to make your eyes squint and to wiggle your ears. If I ever did it when I was a little boy, I was told to be careful or my face would stay that way, if the wind changed. I didn't really believe that, but if you look at the faces of some grown-up people, it could be true. We look sometimes as if we had been caught making a face when the wind changed. Actually we've just got into the habit of looking sulky and bad-tempered and depressed.

All you boys and girls have nice faces but you don't get any credit for that. It is just the way God made you. As you grow older your face will be very largely what you yourself make it. You will be to blame if it looks cross and miserable. If you want to grow up looking pleasant and happy and good, the only way to do it is to be pleasant and happy and good. And the way to do that is to learn from Jesus, the best who ever was. He has promised that if we learn from him and think much of him, we shall be like him at the last, and nobody could be nicer than that.

———— · ————

Liquorice Allsorts

I have some things in a box in my hand where you cannot see them, girls and boys. Would you like them? Perhaps first you would like to know what they are. Listen carefully and I will tell you what they are made of. Sugar, Treacle, Flour, Glucose, Gelatine, Cornflour, Tri-calcium Phosphate, Sodium Alginate, Tri-sodium Citrate. They do not sound a bit nice, do they? But if you do not want them, I'll have them for myself. For, when you mix all those nasty-sounding things together, do you know what you get? Liquorice Allsorts! So it does not do to be put off by a list of ingredients. Even things which do not sound very pleasant are needed to make up something good.

Life's like that too. It is made up of all sorts of things – ingredients, we call them – some easy, some hard, some enjoyable, some painful: going on holiday and going to school; going to parties and going to the dentist; laughter and tears. We may think we would like it if life were all fun and games, all parties and holidays, but we wouldn't really. We would soon become very bored indeed and long to get back to school. So don't try to dodge away from all the hard and unpleasant things in life. They all have their place. The best life that was ever lived, the life of Jesus, had sorrow in it, and pain and difficulty. Jesus will help us, if we ask him, to take our share of difficulty and pain without complaining.

Jesus himself said, "Whosoever will come after me, let him deny himself, and take up his cross, and follow me." *(Mark 8.34)*

My! How you've grown

Grown-ups say a lot of silly things. One of the silliest is when they meet you after some time and they say, "My, how you've grown!" What do they expect? That you'll get smaller and smaller until you're a baby again? Well, let me be silly now and say to all of you, "My, how you've grown in the years I've known you!" Of course, some of you I haven't known for very long, but you have grown as well.

Even grown-ups go on growing. I've grown a little greyer of hair, a little thinner on top, a little thicker in the middle.

The truth is, we're all growing all the time. Even since you came into church your fingernails have grown a little longer, and so has your hair. We have all grown a little bit older.

Every day we are growing, that's for sure. What matters is *how* we're growing. Are we growing kinder, truer, more loving every day? Above all, are we growing more like Jesus? For really that's the only thing that matters – that every day we should grow a little more like him till finally we are just like him.

St. John said, "We know that when Christ comes we shall be like him." *(1 John 3.2)*

That's what we should wish for ourselves and for one another most of all.

A MISCELLANY

Swords into ploughshares

On the Ayrshire coast there is a pretty village called Ballantrae. It is a very ancient place and it has the ruins of an old castle called Ardstinchar Castle, so called because it is built on the banks of the river Stinchar. Once upon a time the people who lived on the opposite banks of the river were always fighting each other. Actually they were relatives, they all had the same clan name of Kennedy, but this just made their wars all the more shocking. It was from one of these families that President Kennedy's ancestors came.

One day the one family of Kennedys attacked the castle of Ardstinchar and set it on fire. It was completely destroyed, only the walls remaining. Those who lived in the castle thought of rebuilding it to carry on the war, but finally they decided that they just would not bother. They made up their minds that, for the future, they would learn to live in peace. They took the stones of the castle and with them they built a bridge over the Stinchar so that the people could come to know each other better, and to like each other, and to live at peace with each other. That was, of course, the only sensible thing to do. So if you ever go to Stranraer by bus or car from Glasgow, you will pass over the bridge that was built out of a castle.

That was what Isaiah meant when he said that the day would come when men would turn their swords into ploughshares. That was what God himself did once. The cross of Christ was a cruel, cruel thing, but God decided to make it a sign of his love to men and of his pardon.

A castle into a bridge, a sword into a plough, and a cross into a crown. That is what love can do.

Give your heart to Jesus

You'll maybe not believe it, girls and boys, but people are sometimes very cruel to me. For example, someone said to me not long ago, "Keep your eyes skinned." That didn't sound very nice to me, so he said, "You know, keep your eyes peeled." That didn't sound any better. I don't mind peeling an orange or skinning an apple, but it would be awful to take your eyes out and try to peel or skin them. So don't you try it.

Well, I had just about got over thinking of that when someone else said to me, "Be sure to keep your mouth buttoned up." My mouth buttoned up! Imagine a little row of buttons along your top lip and some buttonholes along the bottom one. That wouldn't feel very nice, would it? But worse was to come. "Keep your ear to the ground," someone told me. There I was with my eyes skinned and my mouth buttoned up, lying down on the damp cold earth with my ear to the ground. To crown it all somebody else said, "Be sure to keep your nose to the grindstone." Poor minister! Eyes peeled, mouth buttoned up, ear to the ground and nose to the grindstone. I was in a proper mess.

Well, luckily none of these people really meant me to do any of these horrid things to myself. All they wanted me to do was to look carefully and listen closely, keep my mouth closed, and remain busy.

So when I ask you to give your heart to the Lord Jesus Christ, I don't want you to go into your chest and tear out the heart you can sometimes feel beating there. What I want you to do is to learn more about Christ and grow to love him, just as he loves each one of us, and to do what he wants us to do, for that will always be best for us and for everybody else.

Leave your hearts and your nice eyes and your ears and your mouth and your nose just where they are, but use them as Christ wants you to; to do his work in the world and to help other people. That's the way to love God with all your heart.

Oh, for a plumber!

During a spell of frosty weather recently I went to see a lady who is a member of my congregation. No sooner had I rung the bell than I heard her hurrying to the door. She flung it open. When she saw me, her face fell, and, before she could stop herself, she blurted out, "Oh, I was hoping it would be the plumber." When she told me that the water supply in her house had frozen up, then a pipe had burst, and now all the water in the house was turned off, I had every sympathy with her. A minister is all right, but he is not much use at mending burst pipes.

Each of us has his own job to do. There is no sense in going to the dentist when you have shoes to mend, or to the cobbler when you have a sore tooth. But both the dentist and the cobbler are needed in the world, and the minister too. Whoever you are and whether you are big or little, there is something that only you are able to do. As one old hymn says, "There's not a child so small and weak but has his little cross to take, his little work of love and praise that he may do for Jesus' sake." Jesus, when he came to the end of his life, said in a prayer, "I have finished the work thou gavest me to do," and in a passage in St. Mark from which our text comes, he compares himself to a man taking a far journey, who "gave authority to his servants and to every man his work." If we ask him to, Jesus will give each of us something to do for him, something that nobody else can do. "To every man his work." *(Mark 13.34)*

———— · ————

Jesus – the man for all men

Boys and girls, do you always understand everything I am trying to say when I am preaching? I am afraid that, if you are honest, you would have to say, "Not always – at least, not every word."

Perhaps there is no need to worry about that, especially if there are only a few words you do not understand.

A few weeks ago I was in Warsaw. Do you know where Warsaw is? It is in Poland. One Sunday morning, after I had taken a service for the people who speak English in Warsaw, I went to hear someone else preach. His name was Wyszynski. He is what is called a Cardinal, a very important person in the Roman Catholic Church. He had a magnificent voice. I could hear that he was a wonderful preacher, but he was, of course, speaking Polish. I did not understand one single word. Well, that's not quite true. There was one word he used quite often. I had used it that morning when I was preaching. Indeed, I use it in every single service I conduct. Can you guess what that word was? Yes, it was Jesus. In a way, that is the person every sermon is about. There are over one thousand languages in the world, all different, but in every language the word Jesus is the same. For Jesus was born and lived and died, not only to be our friend, but to be the friend of all men and women everywhere. God, our Father, sent his son, not just to be our saviour, but, as St. John once said, "to be the saviour of the world." *(1 John 4.14)*

---------- · ----------

Lost?

Do you ever lose anything, boys and girls? I am sure you do. Had I been in your house this morning when you were getting ready for church, I feel pretty certain I would have heard, "Mummy, I've lost my gloves." "Mummy, have you seen my Bible?" "Mummy, somebody has taken my scarf." At least that is the sort of thing I heard in our house. It is even possible to lose yourself – to wander away from home until you don't know where you are – a horrid experience.

Grown-ups lose things too, of course. I lost something this week. I lost it although I have never seen it. Indeed, nobody has ever seen it. I have got it back again now, but I still cannot see it. Neither can you. If I tell you that you can hear it, you will know what it was I lost. It was my voice.

It is amazing the things one can lose from time to time. It is even possible to lose God, to feel sometimes that there is no one there to listen when we say our prayers, no one to help when we need it most. It is terrible when that happens, and it happens to us all. When it does, we should try to remember one thing. However often or however completely we lose God, he never for a moment loses us. He sent Jesus to look for us and to find us, and Jesus said, "Of them which thou gavest me I have lost none." *(John 18.9)*

---------- · ----------

Take care of your feet, and your soul!

Which bit of you works hardest, boys and girls? When your mother gets tired of cooking and baking, she probably thinks it is your tummy. When you chatter in class, your teacher may say that it is your tongue. I think it is your feet. After all, your neck has only your head to carry, your legs carry your bodies, but your feet carry the lot, head, body and legs. Every step you take, three, four or five stone in weight come thumping down on your poor old feet. You know how tired you can be if you have to carry a basket for ten minutes. Your feet have to bear the whole weight of you day after day, year after year, till the very end of your lives. You really ought to be kind to your feet. They have a lot to bear, and they have to last you a long while. I almost said that they would have to last longer than anything else, but that is not quite true. Your soul, the unseen bit of you, lasts longer. It lasts not only till the end of your life but beyond it – for ever. That is why it is even more important to take care of it than to take care of your bodies, more important to say your prayers and come to church and Sunday School than anything else you do.

Remember what Jesus said, "What shall it profit a man if he shall gain the whole world and lose his soul? Or what shall a man give in exchange for his soul?" *(Mark 8.36-37)*

Nicknames

Do you know anybody called Kerr? Well, that name was first given as a nickname.

It means "left-handed" or "corrie-fisted."

If you have any friends called Cameron, have a look at their noses, for Cameron at first meant "crooked nose." Campbell means twisted mouth. What Gray means I don't know, but nearly all our names were originally nicknames. They seemed to fit the people concerned, so they stuck.

The disciples of Jesus were first called "Christians" as a sort of nickname, but the name seemed to fit so it stuck.

That is the name above all others of which we should try to be worthy, to be worthy of being called Christ's men and Christ's women, Christ's boys and girls, like the disciples.

The boomerang

Girls and boys, you all know the story of William Tell who shot an arrow at an apple resting on his son's head. The other day I heard of a man who shot an apple off his own head, but it was not with a bow and arrow. It was with another sort of weapon. Who knows what it was? I've got one with me in the pulpit. Its a boomerang, and if you use it properly, as aboriginal people do in Australia, you can not only hit something with it, but you can make sure it comes straight back to you afterwards. I've often wondered how an Aborigine gets rid of a boomerang when he's tired of it. Every time he throws it away, it must just come straight back to him. It's a wonderful thing, a boomerang.

But there are lots of things just like it. Every unkind thing you do will come back and hit you sooner or later. Lies are like boomerangs too, and so is selfishness. So also with good things. If you are kind and helpful and courteous to other people, they will be kind and helpful and courteous to you.

Jesus once said, "Whatever measure you deal out to others will be dealt back to you." *(Matthew 7.2)*

---·---

The favourite day

What is your favourite day? I'd like to think that it was Sunday, when you come to church and Sunday School. But maybe it's Saturday when you can lie in bed or play football and hockey. Or Friday, when school is over for the week and it's the night you go to Boys' and Girls' Brigade.

Do you know my favourite day? It's tomorrow. I don't mean Monday, I mean tomorrow. Tomorrow I'm going to get up early. Tomorrow I'm going to work very hard all day. I'm going to be so good-tempered tomorrow, and so kind to everybody. Is that how you feel too?

But you know, Jesus kept on telling his friends not to worry about tomorrow. He wants us to make the best of today. He wants us to start being kind and cheerful and brave today. He wants us to give up our bad habits today. He wants us to give him our obedience and our service, and our love and our loyalty, and to give them today.

For of course, there is one great trouble about tomorrow. It never really comes. It is always ahead of us.

So let's make today our favourite day. Let's begin afresh with Jesus today.

Be sincere

Do you know what "sincere" means? Honest, candid, genuine, truthful. Nowadays that is what it means, but once upon a time it meant something different. It meant "without wax", "sine cera". Long ago men who made statues or carvings sometimes made mistakes. If they weren't very honest they filled up any little holes with wax. But honest sculptors and carvers wouldn't do that and they were known as "sine cera", without wax.

Do you see what I have in my hand? It is a shepherd's crook or cromach. It was made for me and given to me by a friend of mine who is a shepherd in Argyllshire, and it is very beautifully made. It is quite perfect, or nearly perfect. There is just one thing wrong with it, a tiny little hole in the handle. When my friend gave it to me he showed me the little hole and said, "I could have filled it up with wax, but I did not think it was right to deceive you." That told me that as well as being kind, he was a sincere man, who would not try to deceive.

So as St. Paul says in his letter to the people of Philippi, "Be sincere." Be honest, candid and straightforward to other people and to God. *(Philippians 1.10)*

Blots

In the town of Dumfries, about a hundred years ago, there lived a schoolmaster called John Craik. Recently a friend of mine saw some of the books John Craik had written and he admired his perfect handwriting. But something else my friend saw he admired a lot more. It was an exercise-book which had belonged to one of John Craik's pupils. The pupil could not have been a very tidy little boy, for almost every page had a great big blot on it. I suppose John Craik could have punished the untidy little boy, but do you know what he did instead? He took every one of those blots and added two little wings to it and a little head. He turned the blots into angels.

That was the sort of thing Jesus was always doing, making sick people well and bad people good. He'll do it for us too. He'll turn our blots, the mistakes we make, into angels to tell of his love.

For even the cross on which he died, a cruel and ugly thing, Jesus took and turned into the sign of God's love and mercy towards us all. "Do not let evil defeat you; instead, conquer evil with good." *(Romans 12.21)*

——————— · ———————

Chess

The other day some boys came to the Manse to play chess. They brought their own chess sets with them. After they had gone, we found this little pawn.

There are sixteen pieces on each side in a chess game, sixteen black and sixteen white. Some are big powerful pieces, like the Queen or the Knight. Now, there's only one black Queen and two black Knights, but there are eight black pawns. You might think that one little pawn would never be missed, yet without this little pawn the whole set is spoiled. For in chess every piece counts, and not only in chess. In the family every member matters, even the littlest baby. In the church every man and every woman, every boy and every girl counts.

Sometimes you and I feel that we don't matter very much, but we do matter. We matter to one another and we matter to God, every single one of us.

Jesus once said, "It is God's will that I should not lose even one." *(John 18.9)*

Books ✓

Are you fond of reading? There is no better way of spending a wet afternoon. We've had a lot of wet afternoons recently. I wonder if any of you have got to the stage of saying, "I've got nothing to read."

Well, you wouldn't be able to say that if you lived in the city of Oxford. There is a wonderful library there called the Bodleian Library. It is very famous, and that is not surprising for it has more than two million books in it. You could read a book every day for six thousand years and still not have read them all.

No matter how clever you are, and no matter how hard you try, you can never learn all there is to be learned or know all there is to know about this wonderful world.

And we can certainly never know all there is to know about God. He knows everything that is contained in every book in the world and much, much more.

But although we can't know all there is to know about God, we can know all we need to know. For he has shown us what he is like in the life and teaching of our Lord Jesus Christ.

Self-driven

In most big cities nowadays there are firms which advertise "Self-Drive Cars." We know what that means. Instead of hiring a car with a driver, you may hire one by the day or the week to drive yourself. It is a good enough idea, but it is a silly sort of name – self-drive cars. What if some old lady were to go in and sit down in the passenger seat and say, "Go on, car, drive away, drive yourself." She would not get very far. No car will drive itself. You have to drive it and you have to know where you want to go.

That is true of life, too. A great many people who would not dream of letting a car run out of control, do not trouble to keep control of themselves. They just do what the whim of the moment dictates, and go wherever their feet take them. Yet, without someone in control, a life never gets anywhere at all nor accomplishes anything very much.

That is what Christ meant when he said, "Without me ye can do nothing." It is only if he is at the wheel of our lives that they become full of meaning and direction and purpose.

The lost road

Do you ever have a bad week, boys and girls? I had one not long ago. I just kept on losing things. One day I lost a key and spent ages looking for it before I finally found it. Another day I lost some papers and have not found them yet. While I was searching for them I lost something else, something I wish I did not have but was very sorry to lose. Can you think what that was? Yes, you are right. It was my temper. That is something we can all do without, but are better not to lose.

We can all lose things at times, usually small things, but on the last day of that bad week I lost something seventy-six miles long and about forty feet wide. That can't slip through a hole in your pocket. You have really got to be an expert loser to lose anything as big as that, but I did. Do you know what it was? It was a road. I set out for one town in the car and found myself in quite another. Fortunately, I did not have to turn back too far before I found the right road again. But as you make your way through life, it is better not to lose your way. It can be disastrous. There is only one way not to lose your way in life nor to be lost yourself. That is to follow Jesus Christ, for he said, "I am the way, the truth, and the life." *(John 14.6)*

——————————— · ———————————

Don't be a dummy Christian

When you go into a shop, you expect to pay for anything you receive, but the other day in a shop in Dunblane I got a present – something for nothing. I thought that I would bring it to show you. You can all see what it is. On the front it says, "Finest Chocolate Assortment. 1 lb. net. 454 grammes." 454 grammes always sounds so much more than 1 lb., doesn't it? Do you know what's in the box? Of course you do. Chocolates. Well, you are wrong. There is absolutely nothing in the box, and when I show you the underside you will know why. For stamped plain upon it is the one word "Dummy." That means that it's for display purposes only.

There are people who call themselves Christians who are like that. Their Christianity is "for display purposes only." There they are, in Girl Guide or Scout or Boys' Brigade uniform, in church or in Sunday School, but that's as far as their Christianity goes. Don't be a "dummy" Christian, putting on a show for other people to see. Be a *real* Christian – genuine, true, useful to God and to all who know you. Don't be like those to whom Jesus said, "You appear like good men on the outside – but inside you are a mass of pretence and wickedness." *(Matthew 23.28) (Phillips)*

--------------------- · ---------------------

Salary

What is it that your father brings home at the end of every week, boys and girls – a nice fat envelope with a little window in it? It is a wage, his pay as it is called in some places. If he waits a little longer for it, until the end of the month, it is an even fatter envelope and gets a longer name. It is called his salary. That's an odd word. I wonder if you know what it meant at first? You know what your father receives for all the work he does – lots of money! It would be very funny and not a bit convenient if he were paid in eggs or bread or bananas! Once upon a time, people were not paid in money, they were paid in things. Indeed, they were sometimes paid in something you ate this morning. You would put it in your porridge, if you are a Scot, and in your boiled egg whether you are a Scot or not. Yes, you have guessed it – salt. We don't pay much for salt nowadays, but once upon a time it was very expensive. It was so precious, indeed, that people used it instead of money, and so, when they had done their work they got their salt, or their "salary." When we say that a man is "not worth his salt," we simply mean that he is not worth the pay he receives.

In Christ's time, salt was very precious. That is why he once said to those who loved him, "Ye are the salt of the earth." By that he meant that they were very precious, very useful and very much needed. And if you are Christ's boys and girls, you too are "the salt of the earth." *(Matthew 5.13)*

--------------------- · ---------------------

Think on these things

Girls and boys, I wonder if you remember the nursery rhyme:

"Pussy cat, pussy cat, where have you been?"
"I've been to London to look at the Queen."
"Pussy cat, pussy cat, what did you there?"
"I frightened a little mouse under her chair."

Do you like cats? I do, but I think that this one was a bit silly to waste time frightening the poor little mouse. If I had gone all the way to London and managed to get into Buckingham Palace, I'd have spent my time looking at the Queen, or at the lovely pictures on the walls, or at the beautiful curtains and carpets.

But, you know, there are people just as silly as the pussy cat. God has put us into this wonderful world, with the great mountains and the rivers, the trees and the flowers. He has given us music to enjoy, and books and pictures and all sorts of splendid things. Yet some people spend all their time thinking about money and the things money can buy. Some boys and girls spend all their spare time looking at the silliest sort of programmes on television. Even in church some children, and grown-ups too, instead of thinking about God and his greatness and goodness, and about Jesus and his love, think all sorts of stupid, mean things.

St. Paul once said, "Whatsoever things are true, honest, just, pure, lovely, of good report; if there be any virtue and if there be any praise, think on these things." *(Philippians 4.8)*

And that's good advice. Above all, think about Jesus and what he said and did. If you do there will be no room in your minds for anything mean or cruel.

Seeking to save

Does the same thing happen in your house on a Sunday morning before church as happens in ours? The air is filled with cries of, "Mummy, where's my coat?" "Mummy, where's my Bible?" "Mummy, where are my gloves?" If you do behave like that, your mother probably says to you what mothers have been saying for a long time, "Don't just shout, look for your things yourselves."

The other day I met a man whose whole life has been spent looking for something he didn't want to find – and he never found it. It was a man I met in a train, and that was what he told me when I asked him what his work was; looking for something he didn't want to find. There's a conundrum for you. I couldn't guess what he was and finally he took pity on me and told me that he was a fireman in a coal mine. His job for forty years had been to search for the deadly firedamp which spells disaster and death to miners. All his life he had searched and searched. Naturally, he hadn't wanted to find such a thing, and he had been fortunate enough to be in a mine where none had ever appeared.

He made me think of all sorts of other useful people who look very diligently for things they don't want to find. When the doctor listens to your heart or lungs, he is hoping that he will find nothing unusual. When the policeman walks his beat, he doesn't really want to find a burglar, unless there happens to be one there. **A lifeguard on the beach is employed to rescue people from drowning, but if nobody gets into difficulties he is better pleased.**

I think that lots of people have the wrong idea about Christ. He is always seeking us to find us. Many people seem to think that he is trying to catch us out, to deprive us of some good thing or to condemn us for doing some bad thing. That is just not so. St. John tells us why Christ came into the world long ago and why he still comes to us. "God sent not his son into the world to condemn the world; but that the world through him might be saved." *(John 3.17)*